"I think this will become the key book on mobilising the local church for evangelism in the English-speaking Western world over the next ten years. It's short (I read it in one sitting). It's crystal clear on the essential stepping stones we need in place for an evangelistic culture in the church. It's realistic about the difficulties as we seek to mobilise the church and individuals. And it's clear that Christ is the treasure we hold out. The authors have spent decades getting their theology and practice clear—we need to take advantage of their hard-won wisdom."

RICO TICE, Founder, Christianity Explored Ministries;
Author, *Honest Evangelism*

"For as long as I have known Doug and Jeff, they have shown a passion for reaching the least and the lost in their own communities. As faithful Christians in healthy churches, we are to work together to reach the unreached. When we do that, our church will be, by the grace of God, a soul-winning church."

MATTHEW SPANDLER-DAVISON,
Ministry Director, Practical Shepherding

"North America and Europe are the two continents in the world where Christianity is declining. We desperately need existing churches and new church plants to experience a renewed passion to engage cities with the gospel and reach the unreached, and so I am so thankful for this book, which takes a deep dive into the word and will inspire a new generation of churches to join in Christ's mission of seeking and saving the lost. I highly recommend this resource to anyone wanting to join in God's activity of expanding his kingdom locally and globally!"

VANCE PITMAN, President, Send Network;
Founding Pastor, Hope Church, Las Vegas

"This book is not merely a manual on evangelism; it is a heartfelt plea to embrace our role as ambassadors of grace and agents of transformation. Whether you are a seasoned pastor or ministry leader or someone seeking to step out in faith for the first time, this book will inspire and empower you to make an eternal difference in the lives of those around you."

DWAYNE R. BOND, Lead Pastor, Wellspring Church, Charlotte, NC;
Director of Pastoral Care at Acts 29

"I love the tone of this book! It's hopeful, inspiring, and so practical. Evangelism can cause fear in the heart of every Christian, but this book provides motivation and joy, not guilt or shame. The biblical wisdom and tangible application offered on these pages will—if you let them—change your approach to evangelism, the culture in your church, and maybe even your city, if the Lord allows. May God use this book, and may he use us!"

JEN OSHMAN, Director of Women's Ministry, Redemption Parker, CO; Author, *Cultural Counterfeits* and *Welcome*

"Every godly pastor and planter wants their church to have a genuine gospel-sharing culture that sees souls regularly being won for Jesus. But for some leaders, it seems like a pipe dream, or it's an area that just doesn't seem to get any traction or something that seems to drop down the priority list. It's because of this reality that I am so thankful that Jeff and Doug have written *The Soul-Winning Church*. It's clear, gracious, and challenging, and I would encourage every church leader to read it, adopt its principles, and lead their church in the wonderful privilege and honour of sharing Christ with those who are desperate for him."

STEVE ROBINSON, Senior Pastor, Cornerstone Church, Liverpool; Dean, Grimké Seminary Europe; Author, *Serve*

"My childhood pastor used to say, 'The first thing to get cold in your body is usually your feet.' J.A. Medders and Doug Logan remind us that the mission of God belongs to the whole church. The Great Commission is not a special calling for a few 'special forces' in the church; it's something he intends for all of us. *The Soul-Winning Church* shows us how to be a church that lives out that calling."

J.D. GREEAR, Pastor, The Summit Church, Raleigh-Durham, NC; Author, *Essential Christianity* and *Above All*

THE

SOUL-WINNING

CHURCH

J. A. Medders and Doug Logan, Jr.

The Soul-Winning Church:
Six Keys to Fostering a Genuine Evangelistic Culture
© 2024 J.A. Medders/Doug Logan, Jr.

Published by:
The Good Book Company

thegoodbook.com | thegoodbook.co.uk
thegoodbook.com.au | thegoodbook.co.nz | thegoodbook.co.in

Cover design by FaceOut Studio | Art direction and design by André Parker

ISBN: 9781802541151 | JOB-007689 | Printed in India

"There is an evangelism that is genuine ... that means accepting Jesus Christ in reality and not in pretense—an evangelism that carries along with it a brotherhood, that so presents Jesus Christ that men see, and see plainly, what is involved in accepting him."

Francis J. Grimké

This book is dedicated to:

Every church who wants to win souls for Christ.
Every pastor who wants see people born again.
Every Christian who wants to be a fisher of men.

CONTENTS

FOREWORD

by Paul D. Tripp

I live in Center City, Philadelphia, between the Convention Center and the historical sites. Because of where we live, we encounter visitors every day who are trying to find their way around our great city. Even with their phones open to GPS, I often see people who, I can tell, are lost and confused. When I see such visitors, I approach them and ask, "Can I help you find something? I live near here and know the area well." With a look of relief, these travelers most often say, "Oh, thank you! Could you direct us toward...?" I then provide them with a simple set of directions, and they go happily on their way.

If you encounter someone who is lost, you don't look mockingly at them, walk away, or say judgmental things to (or about) them. If you know you can help but ignore them and walk the other way, something is wrong with you. If you're too busy to offer them the help they need, you're too busy. Lost people can't make themselves "un-lost." The very nature of being lost is that you're in a place where you need the intervention of someone who cares enough about your plight to help.

As I've walked the streets of my city, there is a passage that has come to mind again and again. These are the words of Jesus: "For the Son of Man has come to seek and to save the lost" (Luke 19:10). Jesus calls unbelieving, unregenerate people "lost." They don't know who they are, where they are, or where they are going. You and I encounter such people every single day of our lives. The people who stay geographically lost in Philadelphia will just have a bad day, but people who are spiritually lost, apart from the rescue of divine grace, will have an eternity in hell, forever separated from their Creator. How should you see and respond to the lost neighbors, servers, store clerks, bosses, fellow employees, and so on whom you are around daily? Consider Jesus. He wasn't passive, uncaring, or condemning. No, in the spirit of divine grace, he went looking for the lost.

How does God view the lost? I love how the biblical narrative clearly answers this question. Before the foundations of this world were set in place, God had a plan "to seek and to save the lost." Immediately after the sin of Adam and Eve, God announced his commitment to this "seek and save" plan. The bulk of what you read in your Bible is the story of how God harnessed the forces of nature, chose a people for his own, and controlled the events of human history so that out of this chosen people a Messiah would come, and through his life, death, resurrection, and ascension, lost people would be found. But there is more. In the latter part of the biblical narrative, the people of God (that's you and me) are named as the Messiah's ambassadors (see 2 Corinthians 5:20). The only thing an ambassador ever does is faithfully represent the zeal and mission of the King who sent them. This means that God has strategically placed every Christian where they are, and every church where it is, to represent the Savior's message, methods, and character. So our lives don't actually belong to us to invest as we please. Because we are the children of God, we are ambassadors: that is, we have a higher calling than self-provision and personal happiness. Every one of us is called to be a caring, loving, active, gratitude-propelled lost-seeker. Every local church is called to build and sustain a culture of evangelism to the lost.

To be a seeker of the lost, we need to be prepared. What does that preparation look like? Preparation begins with the eyes of the heart. When you see your neighbors, fellow workers, relatives, and the people you walk by when you're out and about, what do you see? Yes, they are clerks, plumbers, Amazon delivery people, Starbucks baristas, aunts, uncles, and bosses, but they are so much more. Each person is a being made in the image of God and is either spiritually lost or has been found by grace. Wherever you are and whoever you're with, there is a moral, spiritual drama being played out before you. Relating to the people around you is more than being polite, respectful, and nice. We are called to be seekers of the lost—that is, to constantly look for opportunities to share with people the dark story of sin and the glorious story of redeeming grace.

I must admit that what I have just described is not natural for me, as it may not be for many of us. I am a project-oriented person. I wake up every morning with an agenda and work hard and fast to accomplish what is in my plan. I tend to live head down, thinking, "I've got things to do," blind to the people around me. So, if I am ever going to be a tool of redeeming grace in God's hands, I need to go on being reminded of that grace. That grace is found in two of our Lord's declarations: "All authority has been given to me in heaven and on earth" and "Remember, I am with you always, to the end of the age" (Matthew 28:18-20). Your Lord rules every situation, location, and relationship where he calls you to be a seeker of the lost. Your Lord never sends you anywhere without going with you. He calls you, not because you have the wisdom, strength, and courage that you need but because he is present with you and offers you his inexhaustible grace, which is fully able to empower and transform you.

Do you live as an ambassador of redeeming grace, and is your church operating as an embassy of redeeming grace? If your answer is "No" or "Not consistently," this book is for you. If your answer is "Yes," this book is still for you. Nothing I have read does a better job of describing what it means for a church to function (from preparation to discipleship) as an evangelistic, lost-people-loving, and lost-people-seeking community. As I read, I was convicted, encouraged, and motivated again and again, and I think you will be too.

Paul David Tripp
January 26, 2024

INTRODUCTION

Imagine a church where members are regularly praying for the conversion of their coworkers and friends.

Imagine a church's members sharing text messages with their small group about evangelistic conversations and asking for prayer.

Imagine a church's teenagers leading their friends to Christ.

Imagine a church having to change the regular order of the worship service because there are so many baptisms.

Imagine a church's membership class being filled with more new converts than new transfers.

Imagine that's your church.

We believe it could be.

That's why we wrote this book.

The Sheep Trade Market

During our years of being in the trenches with church planters and pastors—assessing, training, coaching, mentoring, and resourcing—we have noticed a hard-to-spot sign of unhealth in some churches. The reason it was hard to spot was that these were churches with growing numbers and great pictures on social media—churches that felt things were going well and that looked like they were doing well.

But when we got more detail on the growth, it became clear that most of the growth was transfer growth—Christians leaving one church to join another.

Now, of course there is nothing wrong with a church welcoming in Christians. Mature believers are a blessing to any church. But there is something wrong when a church is *mainly* growing through adding Christians from churches in the area. There is something wrong when a church is functionally content with transfer growth.

That's why we wrote this book. We want to refuse to be satisfied with the sheep trade market. Gaining members from a church down the street, swapping saints, and sharing the pie is not advancing the gospel. In Matthew 28, Jesus calls us to *make* disciples, not *move* them. We want to see a renewal of the missional drive and evangelistic culture in local churches, surrounded as we are by those who are lost without Christ.

We bet that, when you stop to think about it or when someone asks you about it, you want this too.

But we all know how an evangelistic emphasis so easily gets eclipsed in our lives and churches. A healthy local church is a hive of activity. There are a dozen things that need attention. Church leaders are inundated and preoccupied with good things like counseling, budgets, denominational required meetings, discipleship, staff management, and sermon preparation. We get it. We've been there. If church leaders aren't careful, good things— biblical things!—can slowly squeeze out the evangelistic nature of gospel ministry.

We wrote this book to encourage churches, young and old, to recover that evangelistic, soul-winning dimension of their ministry.

Soul-Winning > Evangeli-shame

Evangelism is one of those words that people—pastors, elders, church members—often find difficult to hear. We know we are called to do it, but we struggle to do it. Guilt, shame, and internal sighs of disappointment tend to well up when evangelism is brought up. So we want to introduce a phrase that communicates the same thing but in a refreshing way: *soul-winning*.

Soul-winning is an old word that sounds strange to our 21st-century ears. And it's this kind of strangeness that we need to rewire how we think of evangelism, of sharing and proclaiming the gospel. Evangelism, while a great word that we will use regularly in this book, can come across as a duty, a have-to, a guilt-trip. The oddness of the term "soul-winning" makes us think about what we're really talking about. We are not just reciting facts about an event that happened one weekend in Jerusalem 2,000 years ago so that we can check it off our mental to-do list and feel relieved that we got it done. *Soul*-winning reminds us of the spiritual, eternal, and supernatural elements at work in our evangelism. Soul-*winning* reminds of the ultimate longing of our evangelism—we want to see sinners won to Jesus. We want to see conversions.

Charles Spurgeon, the great Baptist preacher of the 19th century, wrote a book called, *The Soul Winner: Or How to Lead Sinners to the Saviour*. He wrote this book to remind Christians—leaders and laypeople—of their calling to call sinners to look to Christ. "Soul-winning," he wrote...

> is the chief business of the Christian minister; indeed, it should be the main pursuit of every true believer. We should each say with Simon Peter, "I go afishing," and with Paul our aim should be, "That I might by all means save some."[1]

Salvation of sinners is the essence of the work. Soul-winning, like fishing, is the kingdom work of casting the net of the gospel message, through a variety of

---

[1] C.H. Spurgeon, *The Soul Winner: How to Lead Sinners to the Saviour* (Fleming H. Revell, 1895), p 9.

preparations and ways, and seeing who the Lord Jesus draws in.

A Church Culture All about Conversions to Christ

While Spurgeon wrote mainly about personal efforts in winning souls to Christ, we want to talk about *churches* that are committed to the cause and effects of sharing the gospel. *The Soul-Winning Church* is about seeing the whole church culture, not just a handful of leaders and members, committed to seeing people born again. We want to see churches become soul-winning churches.

Maybe your church has tried from time to time to have a fresh emphasis on evangelism. You've made it a common application in your sermons. You've run a Sunday school or midweek course on it. You've held some events for members to invite nonbelieving friends to hear the gospel. But evangelism still isn't getting the traction you had hoped. We'd encourage you to look broader in terms of all your church is, and deeper in your view of discipleship, and longer-term in what you're aiming for.

From our time around the world and around the block, we see six areas that are essential for being a soul-winning, evangelistic church. We believe God can use these keys to foster a culture of evangelism and conversion. A soul-winning church, under the power of God, will be operating in these six areas:

Each key isn't all that groundbreaking. And that's good news. But in our experience a church will tend to be mindful of one or two areas, but not all six. The churches that are paying attention to and active in all six tend to see a lot of fruit. Because these are the silver bullet? No. Because these are the supernatural operations God uses.

So we hope that in these chapters, you may find a new way to do an old thing. You might find that a simple encouragement or a case study from another church at the end of the book changes how your church spreads the gospel. We hope that you will find new angles, thoughts, and practices for sharing the good news in your context. The principles of our book can be applied to any church— mega or small, new plant or historic. What we lay out in these pages can be applied to church in North America or New Delhi and can be used across the whole of a church— including various ministries in the church (kids, students, retired people, and so on).

For a culture like this to take root and spread, we recommend reading this book with a group. You can organize a reading and discussion time with the whole staff team or church leadership and maybe add a few committed church members. Reading together helps set a shared vision, prompt great discussion, and make sure that things actually happen. We've all read books on a certain aspect of church life or ministry which we underlined, and we enjoyed what we read but kept doing what we were already doing. Invite a number of people into learning, processing, and sharing the burden of the church becoming evangelistic.

Our Prayer for Your Church

Our prayer for this little book is that it would have a reviving, inspiring, renewing, and missional effect on our churches. We are praying for God to do a profound work in your church that will reach generations of families in your community. We are praying that this book will not serve as a rebuke or a reminder of past evangelism dereliction. No, we want it to be an invigorating guide that helps foster a new culture in your entire church, so that evangelizing your community is central to your church's existence and every member's life, not merely an add-on or an option.

Imagine a church where the miracle of people coming to Christ is the norm, not the exception. Where space is at a premium and chairs are running short. Where gospel-sharing is a positive, joyful part of the culture—simply a part of what the church does, and loves doing.

It could be your church. It really could.

And it all begins with prayer to the God who saves.

1. WHERE THE HARVEST BEGINS

Pray for Conversions

"Of course."

Is that what you thought when you saw the subtitle of this chapter? Great. To which we'd like to gently ask, "And are you?" Not only your pastoral staff team or your elders (though that would be great) but your whole church—are you praying regularly, specifically, for particular people to come to Christ? In our experience, there can often be a gap between intention and reality. A large part of this book is about that gap.

Maybe, though, your thinking ran more like this: "Well, I know we need to be praying for people to be saved, but the last thing I need right now is more guilt trips and convicting lines about prayer." We aren't here for that. Guilt trips are the devil's doing. We are here to encourage you—to join arms with you and your church.

Or maybe you thought, "Just tell me what our church needs to do." Fair enough. And this chapter is that.

What I (Jeff) want to do in this chapter is both very simple and very supernatural. I want you to feel compelled to pray for conversions—and do it. If you want to actually be an evangelistic church, you will need to be a church that actually prays for conversions. God is the only one who can make them happen. I want us to imagine together what our churches, lives, and baptism calendars could look like if we create a culture of praying for conversions in our churches.

At the end of this chapter, we'll talk about simple and strategic ways in which we can create a culture of prayer for the lost. But action that is effective and sustained comes after inspiration. So, before we get there, I want to exhort us to return to the root, the power, the public secret of revival and renewal in our churches—praying to the God who saves.

Begin with Prayer

My wife Natalie and I love to watch cooking shows. There are not many cooking competitions we haven't watched. And whether we are watching the worst cooks in America or top chefs from around the world, the starting point is always the same. A chef's first step is to get their *mise en place* prepared—French for "everything in its place" (pronounced "MEEZ ahn plahs," though maybe a Texan isn't the best person to guide you on how French should sound). The principle is to get everything together first—pans, boards, pots, skillets—and get everything washed, chopped, diced, peeled, cubed, and ready to go. First things first. Before the chefs start whirling about the kitchen doing the cooking, they prepare.

The *mise en place* of gospel ministry is prayer. Before we rush into *doing*, it is important that we get the first things first. Effective evangelism begins with seeking the Effector of the evangel. Prayer is our first work.

It's worth challenging any "of-courseness" we have when we think about prayer. You may have good books about prayer on your shelves, and your church may have sound doctrine on prayer... but how is your church's experience? How is your church's regular practice in praying for people to be born again? Is there a culture of praying for conversions—for the salvation of sinners? Are these kinds of prayers the habit, rhythm, and expectation of most of your members? If not, it's no wonder we lack supernatural power and fruit. Diminished prayer reveals elevated levels of confidence in our natural abilities in ministry. Infrequent or nonexistent prayers for unbelievers to behold Christ reveal that we've lost our way. We fail to pray for conversions either because we are content with the size of our church or because we are content with ourselves, our approach, and our manufactured man-centered results in aiming to grow. Our desires need to change. And since you are reading this book on being an evangelistic church, I trust you are headed in the right direction. Perhaps the first prayer is to ask God, now, to awaken your own heart for his mission. Ask him to give you fresh eyes, a renewed heart, and an ambition to see people born again.

Thankfully, God has written a prescription to treat a prayerless condition. The Bible is our medicine, correcting our vision, our heart, and our zeal. So, let's look at a few texts in God's word and toss these truths onto the embers glowing in our hearts for the conversion of sinners. Maybe you've become cold over the years, or maybe this passion has been smothered by other legitimate needs in your life, your family, or your church. Sparks can fly again. Light and heat will issue from the crackling, popping, and heat of God's word.

The Heart of Jesus

Jesus looked out over Jerusalem and longed for its people to turn to him. In fact, he wept because of the city's lostness (Luke 19:41). We are to imitate our Lord and look at our cities, communities, and neighborhoods with a longing for them to know the grace of God. We need to be swept up by God's passion to forgive, to redeem, to bring to life. We must see, hear, and feel Christ's heart for sinners. I'm not aiming to convince you that prayer for God to save people is necessary. Rather, I hope these words put a fire in your belly. I believe these words from God can bring you to put your coffee down and put your hands together, as your heart fires and you can do nothing other than pray, "Save, Lord!"

Jesus Told Us to Pray for the Harvest of Souls

As Jesus went through cities and villages proclaiming the gospel of the kingdom, he looked at the crowds and swelled with compassion. His heart was moved toward them because they were lost, "like sheep without a shepherd" (Matthew 9:36). From this heart of compassion Jesus turned to his disciples, and turns to us now, to say:

> *The harvest is plentiful, but the laborers are few; therefore pray earnestly to the Lord of the harvest to send out laborers into his harvest.*
>
> (Matthew 9:37-38, ESV)

We glean three vital truths from our Lord's words about a harvest of souls:

1. The harvest of sinners coming to Christ is plentiful. This is not a hopeless task.

2. Those willing to be about the work of evangelism are fewer than the opportunities. Jesus wants us to labor for soul-winning—for conversions in evangelism.

3. We must pray *earnestly*.

How we need the word "earnestly" to define our prayers! Our Lord isn't calling for a one-time prayer, or a quick oh-yeah-by-the-way prayer, for the saving of sinners around us. The word *earnestly* means pleading, begging, imploring, entreating, and doing so urgently. This kind of prayer is intense and continual. The Savior says to us, *Pray urgently. Offer pleading prayers. Beg the Lord of the harvest.* We pray not only for the sending of the workers but for the fruit of the work. We earnestly pray that the laborers don't come back empty-handed but with a reaping of those redeemed by the blood of the Lamb. Does *earnestly* capture how you pray for the conversion of the lost? It can today. When we pray this way, our heart aligns with God's. This is God's desire.

Jesus Said to Go Ahead and Ask

Jesus green-lights prayers that are persistent, intense, and marked by a "shameless boldness" (Luke 11:8). In the Sermon on the Mount, Christ tells us to ratchet up our prayers and be ready to receive what we ask for. So when it comes to praying for people to be born again, we should ask for it, seek it, and knock on the throne-room's door.

> Ask, and it will be given to you. Seek, and you will find. Knock, and the door will be opened to you. For everyone who asks receives, and the one who seeks finds, and to the one who knocks, the door will be opened.
>
> (Matthew 7:7-8)

Jesus gave a whole parable to teach us "to pray always and not give up" (Luke 18:1)—the story of a widow seeking justice from a terrible, ungodly judge. The judge ignored the widow's pleas, but she had no quit in her. So this judge realized that "because this widow keeps pestering me, I will give her justice, so that she doesn't wear me out by her persistent coming" (v 5). *If this is how an ungodly judge operates,* Jesus is saying, *imagine how eager your loving heavenly Father is to answer his children who ask him to do his will in and through them, and to bring people on earth to faith!*

If we are honest, some of the language Jesus uses about prayer makes us uncomfortable.

> *Whatever you ask in my name, I will do it so that the Father may be glorified in the Son. If you ask me anything in my name, I will do it. (John 14:13-14)*

We aren't sure how to safely handle his *whatever* and *anything*. We aren't sure how to explain it. And that is the point. We are called to believe it—and pray it! That is faith. We can caveat *whatever* and *anything* till we paint over the power, excitement, and invitation to truly pray. Our prayers suffer from death by a thousand qualifications. But here's what I know: we should have zero hesitation and skepticism in asking Jesus to draw sinners to himself through our prayers. He loves to answer these prayers.

God Is Pleased with Our Prayers for Conversions

As the apostle Paul coaches and instructs Timothy, his spiritual son in the faith and in ministry, we see a non-negotiable dimension of every church's ministry— praying for people to be born again.

First of all, then, I urge that petitions, prayers, intercessions, and thanksgivings be made for everyone, for kings and all those who are in authority, so that we may lead a tranquil and quiet life in all godliness and dignity. This is good, and it pleases God our Savior, who wants everyone to be saved and to come to the knowledge of the truth. (1 Timothy 2:1-4)

The late theologian Eugene Peterson rendered the first verse of this passage in a refreshing and striking way: "The first thing I want you to do is pray. Pray every way you know how, for everyone you know" (2:1, MSG). My less eloquent summary: pray for conversions. Why do we pray for our leaders' decisions to allow us to live peaceful, quiet, godly, dignified lives? Because this gives us maximum opportunity to show and speak of Christ to those around us, and "God ... desires all people to be saved" (ESV). Do your prayers show that this same desire lives in you, too?

It's striking that Paul says these words at all to Timothy. He must have known that Timothy, and the church he was leading, needed a reminder of what God's great desire is. It's no surprise that we need it too. God's word *urges* us to pray for the salvation of sinners. When we ask God to save a friend, or a family who have started visiting our church, or a gender-confused student who works in the local coffee shop, we are praying in line with God's desire. We are asking God to do what he already wants and loves to do. "Save, Lord. Bring her to a knowledge of the truth." God is pleased with the church whose desires mirror his, and who therefore pray individually and corporately for the salvation of people.

Make it a Culture

Culture is one of those words that can be tricky to define and itemize. Culture is the shared experience of the church—the stated and (crucially) *lived* values of the church. It's not just the core values listed on the website—it's what is actually lived, felt, celebrated, pursued, realized, and protected in the life of a church body. Culture is the vibe, ethos, and spoken and unspoken communal commitments of a church. Here are some ways to create a culture of praying for conversions in your church.

Make Every Meeting a Prayer Meeting

I'll talk more about church prayer meetings at the end of this section, but take your pastor/elder meetings and turn part of them into mini-prayer meetings. Take the agenda of your meeting and write on it, "Pray for conversions." How many meetings do you have a year? 12? 24? 45? These prayers will stack up before the Father, month after month, year upon year. Persistent, hungry, pleading prayers for God to save sinners. I believe he will answer. Believe together that he will. So far as you are able, ensure that the leadership culture of your church (or home group, or children's ministry, or whatever) is one of praying for conversions.

As you pray for conversions, I'd like to suggest you pray for a specific number of people to be converted. That may seem strange, but let me explain.

Back in my first year of pastoring a dying church, I was mentored by a wise and proven leader. In one of our sessions, he asked me, "Jeff, how many people are you asking God to save this year?"

I gulped and sheepishly replied, "Uh, I don't know? I mean, I guess however many he wants to?"

He paused. "Jeff, why wouldn't you pray for a specific number?"

I paused. "I don't know; it feels strange."

"Sure," he acknowledged, "but wouldn't it be amazing to celebrate and praise God if and when he specifically answers that prayer?"

He had a great point. And he went further.

"Jeff, let's think and talk about why you are hesitating to put a number out there. Why do you think that is?"

I knew right away.

"I'm fearful. If we don't hit that number, I will think I'm a failure. Honestly... I have little faith."

And there it was—my words coming from the overflow of my heart. I repented of my lack of faith, and we both committed to pray for 20 people to get baptized that year. God heard our prayers—19 were immersed. (This was the perfect number to simultaneously teach me that prayer is powerful and to keep me humble.) Twenty baptisms was a bold prayer for a church on life support. Do you need to upsize your prayers?

Create a culture of praying for conversions in staff meetings, meetings about specific ministries, and small-group gatherings. Don't let the presence of coffee in your meetings be more consistent than praying for conversions. Pray for people by name, pray for the Sunday service, pray for neighbors, pray for coworkers— bring names and situations to Jesus and ask the Spirit to move. And do this every week, at every meeting, at every opportunity. Culture is built by repeated actions. Work towards "We pray for God to save people" being a part of your church's culture.

Think about Every Ministry

Don't overlook your existing ministries as opportunities for saving sinners. Children's and student ministries are not Christian daycare centers or babysitting services with a Bible in the room. They do not exist to give parents a break. These environments are part of God's harvest.

If you are a teacher in third-grade Sunday school, pray for these precious children to meet Jesus. Pray for them weekly. As you teach the lesson, talk about the gospel, sin, hell, and trusting Christ as personal belief in the Lord Jesus. If you are a children's minister, I know your job is filled with recruiting, scheduling, and administrative work. But make time to bring these children's names before our Father, asking him to bring them to life in Christ. Cast a vision for your children's teachers to pray for conversions. Send emails to remind them to pray, to report on how God is moving, and to give encouragement to keep laboring in the Lord's harvest.

High-school student ministries may be the most challenging they have ever been. The advent of smartphones, social media, and the confusion over sexuality and gender should not cause us to panic, though. It should move us to pray. Sovereign grace is never outmatched and the Holy Spirit is never outmuscled. We cast these cares—these students' souls—onto Christ.

Have More People Praying More on Sundays
Prayer should saturate the Sunday service. The preacher should have prayed beforehand and should be praying during the service, longing for God to save through the preaching of the gospel. The church should be praying, looking for the Spirit to move. It's not uncommon for a church to have a pre-service prayer time, but it's also not uncommon for this to be more of a service run-through than talking to God about raising souls from the dead. Pray for miracles. We have a God who can deliver them.

I'd encourage you to expand the pre-service prayer time to include more than staff or the people who are involved up-front in the service. Make this another space where everyone is welcome to gather and ask God to send the fresh wind of the Spirit. Put it on the calendar. Invite members, small-group leaders, students, and senior saints. The agenda is simple: pray for conversions. When Charles Haddon Spurgeon, the great Victorian preacher, was asked about the secret to his ministry and the thousands converted through it, his answer was clear: "My people pray for me." And Spurgeon prayed himself, too. Look at the ways Spurgeon publicly prayed in the Sunday service for the conversion of unbelievers:

Lord, convert our friends that still remain unsaved.

Take hold of some that are especially set against Thee, some that are very bold spirits even in sin, thorough-hearted in their wickedness—convert such now!

One more prayer: it is, convert those who sit with us from Sunday to Sunday and are unconverted.

Revive the Prayer Meeting

Spurgeon's church, the Metropolitan Tabernacle, contains an archive of his sermon notes, meeting minutes, and letters he wrote to his church. On a research trip there, I came across a letter I'll never forget.

Spurgeon was resting and recovering in Menton, France. He was in great need of rest from the mental, spiritual, emotional, and physical demands upon him in London. He wrote to his church and closed the letter encouraging them and trusting that the Holy Spirit would anoint, comfort, and strengthen them. He signed off, "Yours in Jesus, C.H. Spurgeon." And then he scribbled a single sentence in the bottom left corner of the letter, with an emphatic double-underlining:

Keep up the prayer meetings.

This may be one of the most piercing things I've read about prayer, because the prayer meeting is typically the most canceled and least well-attended event on a church's calendar. As soon as a scheduling conflict appears either in the church's calendar or in a member's weekly calendar, the prayer meeting tends to lose.

The Scripture says to pray without ceasing, not to cease praying (1 Thessalonians 5:17, ESV). So ask some honest questions about your approach to prayer meetings.

- Does your church have a prayer meeting?

- What does it say if the prayer meeting is the least well-attended meeting?

- Is there more teaching, singing, and church updates than actual praying at your prayer meeting?

- Are you passionate about the prayer meeting, or is it thrown together an hour before?

I wonder if our struggles with prayer meetings are because they are one of the few gatherings that don't appear to be doing anything for us. It's just praying. But that's a lie from the devil. "You can do nothing without me," says Jesus (John 15:5). Outside your Sunday gathering, the prayer meeting is the most, not the least, important meeting you have, and inside the prayer meeting, prayer is the most crucial element of what you do. Believe that, live that, and teach that.

If you need to start or revive your prayer meetings, here are a few things to consider:

1. *Pray more.* Don't let teaching and singing override the purpose of the gathering. Start with a song and some quick instruction, and begin praying.

2. *Vary the voices.* Let others pray, to keep it fresh. Get smaller groups praying together, everyone praying with a leader, popcorn prayers... get everyone involved.

3. *Try a different time.* If your current slot isn't working for your people, try another one.

4. *Start small.* Maybe begin with 30 minutes of praying for one thing. Begin with whoever attends, and watch it grow over time.

5. *Lead.* Leaders must demonstrate their passion and commitment to the meeting. Your excitement is infectious. And so is any indifference or disengagement.

6. *Celebrate.* God answers prayers. Share with people how the prayers they prayed at last month's

meeting were answered. There's nothing like seeing God answer prayer to get people praying.

7. *Clarify expectations.* Ask your members to make prayer meetings non-negotiables in their week. And share with them why prayer matters and why prayer is amazing—aim for them to come to pray not because they should but because they want to.

Let Us Pray...

In closing, here are more logs for your heart-fire. As you seek to foster a culture of praying for conversions with leaders, staff, small groups, students, and those in the prayer meeting, you could use these verses in your time together (and you could also use a "Liturgy for the Lost" such as the one in the Appendices on page 165). I've found so much help in praying a passage, riffing on it like a jazz band. Here is the note, the key, the beat, and let's pray together.

Now to him who is able to do above and beyond all that we ask or think according to the power that works in us—to him be glory in the church and in Christ Jesus to all generations, forever and ever. Amen.

(Ephesians 3:20-21)

"We know you are able to convert more people than we could even ask or imagine—so do it for your glory, God! Blow us away with your power to save! Bring more generations of people praising you."

"Today salvation has come to this house," Jesus told him, "because he too is a son of Abraham. For the Son of Man has come to seek and to save the lost." (Luke 19:9-10)

"Lord, we know you can bring salvation today. You came to seek and save the lost. So, Jesus, it is no stretch to ask you to convert the lost. Save students, save our neighbors, save our families. Save these specific people, Lord..."

Pray at all times in the Spirit with every prayer and request, and stay alert with all perseverance and intercession for all the saints. Pray also for me, that the message may be given to me when I open my mouth to make known with boldness the mystery of the gospel. For this I am an ambassador in chains. Pray that I might be bold enough to speak about it as I should.
(Ephesians 6:18-20)

"Father, you know our weakness. We often aren't paying attention to the opportunities to talk about Jesus. Help us see. Make us bold in evangelism. Give us the words we need to make your gospel known."

Devote yourselves to prayer; stay alert in it with thanksgiving. At the same time, pray also for us that God may open a door to us for the word, to speak the mystery of Christ, for which I am in chains, so that I may make it known as I should. Act wisely toward outsiders, making the most of the time.
(Colossians 4:2-4)

"Lord, we don't want to give up praying. Fortify our present zeal for future faithfulness. Open a door of effective gospel fruit. Bless the preaching of the word, causing people to be born again. Give me an open door with my coworker. Let the little children clearly hear the gospel this Lord's day—please bring them to you, Jesus."

I will take you to be my people, and I will be your God, and you shall know that I am the LORD your God, who brought you out from under the burdens of the Egyptians. (Exodus 6:7, ESV)

"Lord, take those around us to be your people. Bring them to know that you are the Lord! Redeem people from their burdens, sins, and spiritual slavery."

I will also sprinkle clean water on you, and you will be clean. I will cleanse you from all your impurities and all your idols. I will give you a new heart and put a new spirit within you; I will remove your heart of stone and give you a heart of flesh. (Ezekiel 36:25-26)

"Lord, free people from their idols, cleanse them from their sins, and make them new by the Holy Spirit. Make them a new creation, Lord. We cannot do this alone; but you can do anything."

I will make you as a light for the nations, that my salvation may reach to the end of the earth.

(Isaiah 49:6, ESV)

"Father, use our church! Use the preaching, conversations, good works, love, and evangelism as part of your plan for your salvation to reach the ends of the earth—and the end of our street, our neighborhood, our city, and our friends. Lord, let your salvation reach the end of this sanctuary and the end of the children's and student ministries."

Seek the LORD while he may be found; call to him while he is near. Let the wicked one abandon his way and the sinful one his thoughts; let him return to the LORD, so he may have compassion on him, and to our God, for he will freely forgive. (Isaiah 55:6-7)

"Lord, you are great and merciful, willing to pardon sinners who call upon you. Father, bring people to surrender their ways and collapse into your compassionate heart."

In their case, the god of this age has blinded the minds of the unbelievers to keep them from seeing the light of the gospel of the glory of Christ, who is the image of God. For we are not proclaiming ourselves but Jesus Christ as Lord, and ourselves as your servants for Jesus's sake. For God who said, "Let light shine out of darkness," has shone in our hearts to give the light of the knowledge of God's glory in the face of Jesus Christ. (2 Corinthians 4:4-6)

"Father, our great adversary has hindered the sight of unbelievers, but you can cause them to see! The light of the gospel can shine up on them! Gracious God, shine in their hearts, let them see Jesus—crucified and raised for them. Convert them, Spirit."

I tell you, there will be more joy in heaven over one sinner who repents than over ninety-nine righteous persons who need no repentance ... I tell you, there is joy before the angels of God over one sinner who repents.
(Luke 15:7, 10, ESV)

"Let the joy roll, Father! Let the angels celebrate the conversion of a sinner this morning. Bring repentance and conversions today, King Jesus."

A genuinely evangelistic church is genuinely praying for conversions. God is the one who saves, and God wants to use his people in his mission. So often, we have not because we ask not—so foster a culture of asking God, again and again, to cause people to be born again. Pray that in a year's time, the idea of actually praying for conversions would be met by any and every member of your church with a heartfelt, based-on-reality, non-complacent "Of course."

2. BEFORE YOU SAY, "GO AND SHARE YOUR FAITH"

The Posture of an Evangelistic Church

We need to rid ourselves of the Nike method for making our churches evangelistic.

We think that, if we tell them to, people will "Just Do It."

But let's inspect what we expect. How many times has evangelism been an application, or the only application, of the Sunday sermon? A lot, I'm sure.

What results have you seen?

For most of us, if we are honest, the answer will be: not many. Why is that? Well, we can tell believers what to do all day long, but just telling them to share the gospel does not form people into the kind of Christians who naturally, happily, and sacrificially evangelize.

There is more spiritual formation needed to become an evangelistic church than simply telling people to "just do it."

Here's why: when we exhort people to share the gospel, it is like asking them to run a marathon as they lie on their couch with a cheese plate. Their response? Either "I'm not ready for that" or "I should do that—but I don' think I can." Evangelism is not something we can bolt onto the church by barking out "Share the gospel" in a sermon or by running a gospel-explaining course. It is something that bubbles up from a vibrant walk and life with Christ and his church. We need to be excited, not just equipped or exhorted.

If you want your church to witness effectively, lead toward a posture in everyday life that will lead to your members wanting opportunities, having opportunities, and taking opportunities. After all, there's nothing more odd (and ineffective) than someone dropping the gospel on a friend who has never seen the gospel make the slightest difference to how that Christian lives, talks, argues, reacts to setbacks, and so on. And there's nothing more natural (and effective) than someone sharing the gospel with a friend who has seen the way that Christ makes a difference in all kinds of ways to them.

So, rather than thinking that to have an evangelistic church we need only encourage our people to go and evangelize, maybe we need to ask: Are we forming the *kind of people* who evangelize? Is our discipleship forming the kinds of believers in whom evangelism bubbles up, as a natural part of their lives? Let's stick with the scary marathon illustration. If I were required to run a marathon, I would need to become the kind of person who runs marathons. My eating would change (big time). My sleep habits, my schedule, my shoes—a lot of things in my life would need to be recalibrated. And when it comes to being an evangelistic church, there are at least eight postures that give rise to an evangelistic people—eight attributes that will foster an evangelistic church. As you read, whatever position you hold in your church, think, "How well am I modeling these to my church by my conduct and life?" And if you have any teaching responsibility of one kind or another, ask, "How can I be fostering these in my church through how I teach, in what I say?"

A Holy Church

As Paul instructs Timothy about the kind of gospel worker God uses, he first reminds him that holiness is nonnegotiable. God can use whoever he wants to achieve his purposes, of course. But he loves to use people who are committed to living by and living out the effects of the gospel—who are committed to holiness.

Now in a large house there are not only gold and silver vessels, but also those of wood and clay; some for honorable use and some for dishonorable. So if anyone purifies himself from anything dishonorable, he will be a special instrument, set apart, useful to the Master, prepared for every good work. Flee from youthful

> *passions, and pursue righteousness, faith, love, and
> peace, along with those who call on the Lord from a pure
> heart. (2 Timothy 2:20-22)*

Our usefulness to the Master is connected to our holiness for the Master. Paul is not writing about an elite version of Christianity, as though this life is akin to an Olympic-level marathon runner's approach to life. Paul is writing about normal Christianity—about the race we are all running. Christians need to be reminded that, having been redeemed by the blood of Jesus and made new by the Holy Spirit, their usefulness in evangelism is proportional to them purifying themselves— repenting—from what is "dishonorable."

I love what the word "dishonorable" communicates to us. Sin is dishonoring to the Lord—and to us. Jesus is telling us, *Okay, that sin is so beneath you. As my royal sibling in my kingdom, you are way above that. Don't stoop down to that sin's level. You are seated with me in the heavenly places. Purify yourself from that. Sit with me.* The gospel is ongoing good news for Christians. We can turn from sins because of Christ, the sin-defeater. We can confess, repent, and pursue the holy, God-honoring lives that are now ours in Christ.

Pastors, lead your people toward holiness. Paul is clear: a lack of holiness will result in a lack of usefulness. If we are no different from the world in our attitudes, speech, sexuality, marriages, alcohol, parenting, friendships, and finances, why on earth would the world even listen to us? Hypocrites are not effective evangelists. But holy lives are a living commentary on the power of Christ. Personal holiness matters in personal evangelism. Could that be why people often hesitate in evangelism? Are there dishonorable actions in our lives that would discredit our witness?

Ask: *What "dishonorable," obvious sins do I need to "purify" from my life? What attitudes, actions, and thoughts are dirtying my usefulness and making me a dishonest evangelist? Do we teach enough about sin, repentance, and holiness?*

A Gentle People

> *The Lord's servant must not quarrel, but must be gentle to everyone, able to teach, and patient, instructing his opponents with gentleness. (2 Timothy 2:24-25)*

Secular culture runs on rage. The attention machine of social media generates, curates, and congratulates the cruel. We must lead our people away from the ways of the world because apprentices of Jesus are meant to follow the way of Jesus, and his way toward sinners is gentle.

Yes, Jesus went flipping tables in the temple, making a whip to drive out the money changers. Yes, he gave a super-strong rebuke to the Pharisees in Matthew 23. But let's think about these texts in context—what is Jesus actually doing here? He is rebuking the self-righteous, people who do not believe they are in need of him and who look down on everyone else. Contrast this with how Jesus speaks to people who know they have not got life taped down, who know they need something beyond themselves—the woman caught in adultery, the woman at the well, Peter, Matthew, the lepers, the children, the thief on the cross. In these encounters, Jesus is truthful and kind. The Lord's servants are called to imitate their Master's posture among the unrighteous.

John 8 is a great model for proclaiming Christ to sinners. A woman is caught in her adultery and is dragged into the presence of Jesus. The Pharisees are ready to dole out the punishment. Death. Jesus enters and takes things in a different direction. As he talks and writes on the ground, and straightens up to say, "The one without sin among you should be the first to throw a stone at her" (v 7), the men begin to drop their stones and walk away. Jesus asks the woman, "Has no one condemned you?" "No one," she answers. They are gone. And Jesus says, "Neither do I... Go, and from now on do not sin anymore" (v 10-11).

Jesus shows us two things our churches ought to embody as we engage with the unrighteous—grace and gravity. First, he does not join the condemnation choir, even though he is the only one without sin—the only one who could throw the first stone. He offers mercy and grace in himself. Second, Jesus doesn't minimize obedience and repentance. He commands her to go and live differently.

Jesus is merciful *and* serious. He shows us how to communicate mercy to lawbreakers without minimizing the reality of sin. Compassion is not compromise; it's Christ-likeness. Gentleness does not involve being squishy about the seriousness of sin. It does involve being compassionate toward sinners. Good news ought to be shared in a good way—a gentle way—because this is what Jesus is like and because "gentle speech breaks down rigid defenses" (Proverbs 25:15, MSG).

A church whose evangelism is effective will be one in which its leaders model and preach about being "kind, always showing gentleness to all people," remembering with humility that "we too were once foolish, disobedient, deceived, enslaved by various passions and pleasures, living in malice and envy, hateful, detesting one another" (Titus 3:2-3). Our own personal history with sin teaches us how to treat sinners—with a humble posture. We know what it's like to be ignorant, selfish, and harmful to others, and to give in to our fleshly impulses. Rather than being harsh to or standing aloof from unbelievers, our hearts break for them. God's grace is designed to simultaneously blast us free from unrighteousness and keep us from smacking our heads on self-righteousness. Arrogance is ignorance of God's grace. If a church's leaders are gentle, that church will enjoy a culture of gentleness, and its people will be in the right posture to preach grace to others, even as they treat sin with gravity.

Ask: *Are we making evangelistic connections from the character of Christ for our people? Is gentleness what generally describes our leadership teams? Would people describe me as gentle?*

A Patient and Dependent People

A high view of the sovereignty of God ought to encourage a high dependency on God in evangelism because, no matter how clear or confusing our evangelism is, salvation is up to the sovereign God.

> *Perhaps God will grant them repentance leading them to the knowledge of the truth. (2 Timothy 2:25)*

It's a leader's job to connect the dots between theology and missiology. Doctrine is the foundation of our mission. The fact that God grants repentance and faith should cause us to relax and rest—the pressure is not on the person sharing the gospel. God can, does, and will use a less-than-tidy presentation of the gospel. Our confidence is in the God of the gospel and not in the one who goes out with the gospel.

At the same time, knowing that conversion is in God's hands should also cause us to pray to him and work for him, and then patiently wait on him to bring people to Christ as we keep working to share the gospel. We don't tell the news of Jesus once, feel good about our obedience, and never do it again. We tell the same person again, follow up, pray for them. We tell more people. God's granting of repentance doesn't decrease the quantity and quality of our evangelistic efforts. It should increase the people we share with and the patience with which we share. We can share the gospel freely and trustingly, knowing that conversion solely rests on the action of God. And we can evangelize patiently, not giving up on people, because it is up to God, not them—and certainly not us.

We need to hear the testimonies of people who were not interested in God and wanted nothing to do with Jesus, but Jesus was interested in them. God uses the patient, continual, and committed witness of his people to bring about saving faith. Churches need reminding that we should never count people out. Monica, the mother of the great 4th-century theologian Augustine, prayed for years that her son would become a Christian. At one point in Augustine's *Confessions*, Monica says, "The single reason why I deeply wanted to stay longer in this life was my desire to see you as a Christian."[2] When Augustine was 33, her patient and dependent prayers were answered. Evangelistic churches are trusting and patient under the sovereign hand of God.

Ask: *Does our church connect our theology to our mission? Have we forgotten that God ordains the ends and the means? How am I doing at being prayerfully dependent on the God who causes people to be born again?*

---

2 My paraphrase from Augustine's *Confessions*, translated by Henry Chadwick (Oxford University Press, 2008), Book 9.26.

A People Who Remember Eternity

Then they may come to their senses and escape the trap of the devil, who has taken them captive to do his will.

(2 Timothy 2:26)

Satan is thrilled if our churches solely exist for their current members. He hates churches that are on mission. Evangelism is a battleground of spiritual warfare, and Christ is our commander. Our people need to be prepared for the attacks and schemes of the devil since we are behind enemy lines and recruiting defectors from the devil with the news that Christ conquered Satan and frees sinners from the hell to come.

Hell is real. And people are going there. Pause for a moment and let the reality of hell rest on your heart and mind. The Bible describes hell as eternal torment (Revelation 20:10), a "blazing furnace" (Matthew 13:42), a "lake of fire" (Revelation 19:20), and a place of "outer darkness where there will be weeping and gnashing of teeth" (Matthew 8:12).

I'm convinced that we do not think enough about hell. While we should be eternally and effusively thankful to "Jesus, who rescues us from the coming wrath" (1 Thessalonians 1:10), that does not exempt us from remembering hell. We have neighbors, friends, coworkers, and acquaintances who, as things stand, will face God's wrath (John 3:36). This should be a continual motivator for our evangelism. Do we know the flames are there?

I've been made more aware of hell by my daughter's soccer games (bear with me). One of the parks her team plays at is nestled behind what we call "Trash Mountain." Houston has zero hills—nothing that resembles elevation. But at this park, there is a massive hill of soil that hides the city's trash dump. Most of the city's garbage is tossed behind this mountain, and when the wind is in a particular direction as we watch our daughter play, we are reminded of why we named it Trash Mountain. And every time, I think of Gehenna in the New Testament.

Gehenna, originally the valley of the sons of Hinnom, was a location of idolatry and sacrifices that were burned to the god/demon Molech. Gehenna eventually became the city dump of Jerusalem. "Here the dead bodies of animals and of criminals, and all kinds of filth, were cast and consumed by fire kept always burning."[3] Israelites knew Gehenna. They knew its smell, its heat, its sounds, its horrors. When Jesus used the word Gehenna for hell, he was employing this awful earthly place as an illustration of the wrath to come, solidifying the reality of hell in the minds of those who had ears to hear, eyes to see, noses to smell, and hearts to ache. Let's not talk about hell less than Jesus did or less dramatically than Jesus did. Evangelistic churches are compelled by the reality of hell to tell people about

---

3 M.G. Easton, *Illustrated Bible Dictionary and Treasury of Biblical History, Biography, Geography, Doctrine, and Literature* (Harper & Brothers, 1893), p 280.

the grace of God and how Jesus saves us from the wrath to come.

Ask: *When is the last time I taught on hell? Are we reminding people of the unseen spiritual realm? Is God's wrath real to our people?*

A Bold People

Almost everyone has exercised boldness at some point in their life. Maybe you find it easy to be bold in a restaurant, or when cheering for your team, or when driving on the highway, or when asking for a raise—for most of us, boldness isn't totally foreign. But for most of us, it's foreign to our evangelism. We need to harness our boldness and use it to proclaim Jesus. We need to embody an evangelistic boldness.

While chained in a Roman prison, Paul told the Ephesian Christians, "Pray also for me, that the message may be given to me when I open my mouth to make known with boldness the mystery of the gospel. For this I am an ambassador in chains. Pray that I might be bold enough to speak about it as I should" (Ephesians 6:19-20). Even in chains, boldness was on his mind. Is it on ours? I would imagine that Paul's prayer reminded the Ephesians to be bold with the gospel themselves too. If you are feeling sluggish or timid, ask your small group to pray for your boldness. These kinds of prayers can catch fire.

Boldness isn't brashness. There ought to be a *gentle* boldness among Christians. Bold evangelism talks about hell, sin, judgment, and the supremacy and exclusivity of Christ. Boldness doesn't cut corners on the message. Jesus invites and demands all people to repent, believe, and receive his salvation. Boldness doesn't flinch. Even though the cross and resurrection of Christ are foolishness to the world, bold Christians speak the whole truth and nothing but the truth, so help us, God. But they do it all with gentleness, with love. Boldness is not anger or annoyance.

Boldness generates gospel conversations, and it seizes opportunities. While working on this book, I was at my daughter's physical therapy session and reading a book on the history of evangelism. One of the therapists asked, "What you readin' there, boss?" I thought, *Why is this guy bothering me? I just want to sit here, read this book, and go home and work on my book on evangelism.* And then it hit me: my natural introversion was about to get in the way of a gospel opportunity. In that moment, I wanted to read about evangelism more than actually doing evangelism. I realized this was a moment to be bold. I needed to be bold in conversation and bold against my own temperament.

So I showed him the cover and said, "It's about how the story of Jesus spread worldwide."

"Oh, yeah? Sounds neat."

"Yeah, since Jesus was crucified for our sins and rose again from the dead, everyone should know—and everyone should trust him and be forgiven of their sins. Jesus is still alive today, and that sets him apart from every religion in this world."

Other therapists were listening as we talked about Jesus. Boldness overrides our dispositions. Boldness captures the moment and bends it toward talking about Jesus. Here's what we should learn about being bold—it is something we choose, enact, and become. Boldness isn't an attribute that you either have or don't have. While we may not always feel comfortable with being bold with the gospel, we choose the cruciform way of life and die to our natural ways and live in the supernatural ways of the Spirit.

Ask: *Is our church channeling people's boldness to boycott the world rather than seeking to share the gospel in the world? Is our leadership bold on social media or from the pulpit but not in evangelism? How is my boldness in talking about Jesus among the lost?*

A Hospitable People

We tend to use the word hospitality in a more limited way than the Bible does. In the Bible, hospitality is always seen as kindness to the outsider, the stranger, and the traveler, and provides what they need (Leviticus 19:33-34). It means to see someone in need and to meet their need, whether it is food, shelter, clothes, time, or money. Rather than seeing someone outside of your social sphere and ignoring them, hospitality widens the circle. God commands us to "pursue hospitality" (Romans 12:13), and it is a requirement for elders (1 Timothy 3:2; Titus 1:8). Jesus really wants us to be hospitable, both within our church family and with our wider community. He calls us to open our homes and our hearts—to give food, time, and resources.

Hospitality is an easy-to-reach ministry for the everyday Christian. Evangelistic churches lead their people to see that every Christian has a hospitality ministry. Every member is on the hospitality team. We take that struggling coworker out to lunch and ask how they are doing. We help the neighbor who recently lost their spouse. We take cookies and restaurant recommendations to someone who just moved in, along with a personal invite for dinner and to join us at church. A posture of hospitality puts Christians on the highway for evangelistic opportunities. And leaders set the pace.

Ask: *How does our church understand and embody hospitality? Is it missional? In what ways could I model and help increase our church's kindness to the lost?*

Side-Note: Hospitable Services

When I was pastoring a church in the suburbs of Houston, I invited the pastor and author Jared Wilson to come speak at a men's conference and then preach on Sunday morning. As the service was starting, Jared leaned over to ask, "Do y'all have a worship guide or an order of service sheet?" I shook my head. With a gentle smile, he then said something I'll never forget.

"Oh, so you don't want visitors to know what to expect?"

Touché. And Jared's half-joke, half-provoke made a huge impression upon me. We had missed an opportunity to remove a barrier for non-Christians—an opportunity to help make them feel welcomed and therefore to them being in the best headspace to hear the gospel.

Consider what it must be like for unbelievers who are unfamiliar with church to attend your worship service. It's foreign soil. It's foreign speech. And that's a good thing. Your church, after all, is an embassy of heaven in a very un-heavenlike world. But at the same time, a hospitable church considers their worship services and asks if there is any linguistic or liturgical fog that could be cleared so that non-Christians can see Jesus more clearly.

A welcoming church—a church that expresses kindness to outsiders—will be one that asks itself, "Other than the gospel and what Scripture tells us is essential to do as we gather, is there anything in our service that forms a barrier that we're asking newcomers to climb over? Is there a way to remove that barrier without losing anything that builds people up? Is anything unclear, unexplained, or confusing? Is there unnecessary awkwardness in our liturgy?" A soul-winning church will consider how the entire service worships God and builds up believers and also, as far as possible, is mindful of unbelievers who are present.

A hospitable worship service does not require you to throw out or tone down the gospel and how it shapes what you do. We're to be Christian! Our services should be unashamedly Godward, Christ-centered, and filled with Scripture. Unbelievers don't need to hear secular music being played as they walk in the room—they need to hear songs about God's grace and their need of Christ. Don't give the lost more of the world when they come to church—give them God, give them gospel. Give them what they can't hear, see, or experience anywhere else. But as you do, give them a sense of what is going to happen (an order of service, for example). Think hard about how to be welcoming and warm in the first few moments of the service. Say why Christians do what we do in our services. Take a few seconds to explain a potentially unfamiliar word in a song. Give a brief outline of the Lord's Supper—why we do it, what it is about, who it is for, and how sinners are able to enjoy it.

The gospel is a stumbling block to unregenerate hearts. We must never remove, dress up, or gloss over it. But that same gospel compels us to make it as easy as possible for those unregenerate hearts to hear it.

Ask: *Are there any barriers you have created that you can take down without losing any of the gospel or any building up of your people? Revisit the questions listed on the previous page.*

A Christ-Excited People

We all want our churches to be Christ-exalting. But what about being Christ-excited? Is there a detectable amount of excitement about Jesus in your church? What registers on the excitement graph in your sermons? Is it a particular doctrine? An over-torqued emphasis on obedience—on what we need to be doing for Jesus? Is it a position you love to punch at or a leadership insight you tend to major on?

Do people walk out of your sermons and think, "Jesus is incredible"?

Jesus himself ought to be the most exciting and invigorating aspect of our churches. And that means he ought to be what excites a church's leaders. D.A. Carson puts it like this:

> If I have learned anything in 35 or 40 years of teaching, it is that students don't learn everything I teach them. What they learn is what I am excited about, the kinds of things I emphasize again and again and again and again. That had better be the gospel.[4]

Your people will catch what you have caught. When you are caught up in excitement over Jesus, who he is and what he's done, your people eventually catch up with you. And this fosters an evangelistic church culture because excitement leads to evangelism.

---

4 thegospelcoalition.org/blogs/justin-taylor/carson-people-dont-learn-what-i-teach-them-they-learn-what-im-excited-about/ (accessed March 5, 2024).

Let me demonstrate.

A few months ago, I was introduced to Jeni's Ice Cream. I've had a lot of ice cream in my day (which is one reason why I am not marathon-ready). I grew up close to the Blue Bell Ice Cream factory, and my family helped them with their profits.

I wasn't expecting much when our friends took us to the Jeni's in Houston. I got my three scoops—gooey butter cake, peanut butter with chocolate flecks, and brown butter almond brittle, if you're interested. I took one bite, and instantly I realized that this might be the portal to the third heaven Paul talked about.

Jeni's isn't stingy or skimpy; the flavors were intense, and saturated every bite. The texture is like no other. Since that glorious day in Houston, I've been buying pints of Jeni's as often as I can.

And, on top of that, I tell people about Jeni's whenever I can. I bring it up in conversations. I offer no apologies for talking about how Jeni's is the best ice cream ever.

And you know what didn't happen? The manager at Jeni's didn't tell me to talk about the ice cream. I didn't watch a video on Jeni's website on how to talk to people who think another ice cream is better. Excitement is all I need. I love telling people about good ice cream.

And I love telling people about Jesus and his good news. Here is D.A. Carson again: "Make sure that in your own practice and excitement, what you talk about, what you think about, what you pray over, what you exude confidence over, joy over, what you are enthusiastic about is Jesus, the gospel, the cross."[5]

An evangelistic church will be a Christ-excited church.

Ask: *Am I actually most excited about Jesus—or mainly about stuff that surrounds Jesus or the good things that Jesus brings? Are we doing church in way that shows that Jesus is the nonignorable excitement of the church? Do I teach that Jesus is still good news for believers?*

An Ambitious People

There is nothing is wrong with ambition, if it is Christ-exalting and gospel-spreading. Everyone has goals and ambitions in life, and while there are many sinful ambitions, God is honored by a gospel ambition that seeks first the kingdom of God (Matthew 6:33)—an ambition like that of Paul, who wanted to share Christ with those who had not heard of him (Romans 15:20). There is no better ambition than seeing God glorified in the conversion of sinners. The efforts and effects of our evangelism go on into eternity—and that's why Paul had a gospel ambition.

Paul was so compelled to spread the gospel that he pronounced a woe upon himself if he didn't preach it. "I am compelled to preach—and woe to me if I do

---

5 As above.

not preach the gospel!" (1 Corinthians 9:16). We could likely use a little more *woe to me*. We are too quick to excuse our failures, faithlessness, and fears in speaking the gospel. Let's call our churches—having first called ourselves—to big ambitions for the spread of the gospel. What do you want to see? What are you asking God to do? What gospel ambition will you lead your members toward?

This does take hard work. Most ambitions worth having do. Dallas Willard was right when he pointed out that the gospel is not anti-effort but anti-earning.[6] Read Paul's letters and you are left in no doubt that he worked hard—really hard. He evangelized all over the Roman world. Paul talked about Jesus in almost every setting imaginable—prisons, homes, riversides, Jewish synagogues, lecture halls, Roman government buildings, and more. It is estimated that Paul traveled over 10,000 miles on his three missionary journeys. Let's rid ourselves of any evangel-laziness and repent of small, manageable, easy ambitions. Let's get off the couch and spread the gospel.

Ask: *What is my personal gospel ambition? What is the gospel ambition and prayers of our church? Are we forming the kind of people who have ambition for the mission?*

---

6 Dallas Willard, *The Great Omission: Reclaiming Jesus's Essential Teachings on Discipleship* (Harper Collins, 2006), p 61. Willard put it this way: "Grace is not opposed to effort, it is opposed to earning."

Run with Grace

The legend goes that marathons began when a man named Pheidippides ran from the battlefield of Marathon to Athens to bring the city good news of victory against the Persians. He ran the 26 miles nonstop to deliver the news. The ancient accounts don't record this, but I imagine that Pheidippides had not been a man who had been laying on the couch eating ice cream, but rather one who was living a life that primed him for this good-news run. We have good news to bring of Jesus' victory over sin, the devil, and death itself. Our life, our posture, must be one that primes us for doing that, and that calls our brothers and sisters to do likewise. Let's get our churches running with the news of the grace of God and the victory of Jesus: churches living in holiness, speaking with gentleness, praying in patient dependence, remembering that hell is real, pursuing boldness, exercising hospitality, excited about Jesus and ambitious for his cause. Maybe we are in a marathon after all.

3. SALT AND LIGHT

Preparing for Conversions

Evangelistic churches have to be prepared for anything. People and opportunities come and go. It's important to be adaptable and roll with issues as they come, but it's equally important to be intentional with your preparation. If you lack a plan, you're setting yourself up for unnecessary hardship in the future. To be an evangelistic beacon of the gospel in your city, you must prepare the way with intention so people will be ready to respond to the good news you declare.

At my (Doug's) former church, which we planted in Camden, New Jersey, we did an outreach event called "Community Connect." We invited people in the community to come for a free haircut. We also invited both city firefighters and police officers in the community to attend. They didn't come as an enforcing presence; they came as friends. Children were meeting the cops in their neighborhood in a fun and safe environment. Seeing a police officer is often an adverse experience, but this event helped bridge the gap in our community. We hosted it to help our city, and we did so with intention. We didn't want to bring people together for the sake of philanthropy or politics—we brought them together so that we would do good in the name of Christ. Our good efforts should always point back to his goodness and his good news.

The church desperately needs both good gospel works and good gospel workers for the good news message. The apostle Paul speaks to this in his letter to Titus. He's writing to exhort Titus as his younger friend leads the church at Crete. Within this short epistle, Paul makes a clear connection between faith and practice. Why is this so important? Our faithful obedience to God's word ensures that "in everything" we can "adorn the doctrine of God our Savior" (Titus 2:10).

I want to exhort you and your church to adopt an essential element of being an evangelistic church: good works.

It may seem odd that a short book about evangelism would dedicate a whole chapter to doing good works. But that's exactly why we need it. Good works are not at odds with the good news of Christ's death and resurrection to save us from our sins. Doing good accentuates our declaration. Loving our neighbor flows from the love of God and then points back to the love of God. Good gospel works will come from a good gospel worker who proclaims the good news, because good works prepare the hearer and give a platform to the teller. Evangelistic churches know the place of good works in good news proclamation. As Richard Lovelace said in his classic book *Dynamics of Spiritual Life*, "The church as an instrument of mission may be compared to a cutting tool whose steel shaft is works of justice and mercy, but whose diamond edge is the proclamation of truth."[7] Works and word go together for evangelistic churches.

Salty and Bright Churches

In Matthew 5:13, Jesus calls us the "salt of the earth." This is often misquoted and taken out of context to proclaim our own worthiness and influence. But it's the second half of the verse that's really important. Yes, we are the salt of the earth, but "if salt has lost its taste, how shall its saltiness be restored? It is no longer good for anything except to be thrown out and trampled under people's feet" (ESV). This isn't a platitude; it's a warning.

Salt is one of the most ordinary minerals on earth. We use it to season and preserve food, and it's often used in industrial production. Salt is essential for human survival. This was especially true in the 1st century. People didn't have the modern convenience of refrigerators to preserve their food, so they relied on salt for preservation. They would rub salt on meat or fish to

---

7 Richard Lovelace, *Dynamics of Spiritual Life: An Evangelical Theology of Renewal, Expanded Edition* (IVP Academic, 2020), p 283.

keep it from decaying and push back its use-by date. Salt was an essential part of both preparing food to nourish in the moment and preserving food for nourishment in the future.

But not all salt was created equal. In 1st-century Israel, most salt came from the Dead Sea and had to be purified before use. In its natural state, it included minerals not suitable for human consumption. It had to be refined and purified before it would actually work. If this wasn't properly done, the salt tasted awful and was useless. The process and preparation of salt before using it were highly important.

And the same is true of the salt of the earth.

When Christ declared us righteous, he also commissioned us to this salty work of missional engagement and evangelism. But remember, not all salt is equal. We don't want to be the kind of salt that is good for nothing but being thrown out, walked on, and ignored. Jesus is warning us that it is possible for our effectiveness for the kingdom to be on par with garbage. So how do we avoid being rubbish salt?

Right after using salt as an image for his people, Jesus switches the metaphor, and as he does so, he's answering that question:

> *In the same way, let your light shine before others, so that they may see your good works and give glory to your Father in heaven. (Matthew 5:16)*

Good works that lead to our Father being glorified—that's what effective salt tastes like. Good works are enlightening. Jesus is very clear that our good works have an illuminating power and are crucial in leading people eventually to give glory to God. We need to realize that Jesus is not saying that our good doctrine is the light that we shine. Neither are our buildings, our church services, or our good children's ministries. What is it that unbelievers see? "Your good works." So we must be zealous to shine—to do good works for gospel advancement.

Zealous Like Jesus

Churches that are full of deeply rooted, devoted disciples of Jesus will be zealous for gospel work. As Paul put it in Titus 2:14, because Jesus has cleansed us and made us his own, we're to be "eager to do good works." There should be a zeal and longing for Christians to do good in their communities. We shouldn't be "doing good deeds" because we have to but rather because we can't help but adorn the gospel with our actions. Jesus wants his churches to be people who "learn to devote themselves to good works" (Titus 3:14). Paul uses the word *learn* because it's not natural for us to do good works. Our nature is selfish, cynical, and judgmental. Even in our new born-again nature, we have to *learn* how to be good-works-doing people. The only way we learn is to look to God's word and to God's Word—to the Scriptures and, supremely, to the Son of God whom they reveal.

The more we understand the salvation Jesus purchased for us and the relationship with God that he has brought us into, the more an eagerness to make him known swells in our hearts. If we were once dead in our sin but are now alive in Christ, why on earth wouldn't we strive to see others come to know this saving faith too? Having a gospel zeal means we're about our Father's business— sharing the gospel in word *and* deed, and caring for the least, the last, and the lost.

This is what Jesus modeled for us during his time on earth. When we read the Gospels, we see Jesus' humility, patience, and urgency to spread his kingdom. He does this by word and works. It is striking that right after the Sermon on the Mount (Matthew 5 – 7), Jesus demonstrates the power of the gospel through good deeds connected to the good news. Jesus wrapped up this sermon and immediately showed compassion to a leper and healed him (8:1-4). When a Roman soldier asked Jesus to heal his servant, he did (v 5-13). After healing Peter's mother-in-law, Matthew writes that the people of the city "brought to him many who were demon-possessed. He drove out the spirits with a word and healed all who were sick, so that what was spoken through the prophet Isaiah might be fulfilled: He himself took our weaknesses and carried our diseases" (v 14-16). He fed thousands, healed hundreds, raised people from the dead, and gave time to those whom police officers today classify as "living a high-risk lifestyle."

Jesus demonstrated the kingdom of God even as he declared it.

Two Dangers to Avoid

There are two dangers to avoid when it comes to mercy ministry and evangelism. First, we must not treat mercy ministry as the same as, or as a valid alternative to, evangelism. People need to hear about Jesus crucified and risen to be saved. We pray people will say, "Lord, have mercy on me, a sinner"—it is not enough for them to say, "Lord, your people are good people and make an impact on this community" (though that is a good start). But second (and in our kinds of churches, this is probably the greater danger), we must not treat mercy ministry as optional or a distraction from the real work of the church. No, it was vital to Jesus' ministry, and must be to us. If it weren't, he would have just preached about repentance and salvation and would never have taken time to tell us a parable about a good Samaritan helping his near-death enemy as instructive for loving our neighbors.

Yes, the accomplishment of redemption and the proclamation of the gospel are the major notes of Christ's ministry. He came to destroy the devil's works, give himself as a ransom for many, and proclaim good news to the captives. But the minor keys—essential to his music—are his works of mercy. These acts of mercy flow from the heart of Jesus for people. We must maintain that doing good works is itself good. Every Christian in your church has good works designed by God for them to carry out (Ephesians 2:10). We don't ignore people's needs because helping them "is not the gospel," nor do we care for them simply so we can evangelize them. Christians do good because we love. The late Tim Keller said it well in his book *Generous Justice*: "Deeds of mercy and justice should be done out of love, not simply as a means to the end of evangelism. And yet there is no better way for Christians to lay a foundation for evangelism than by doing justice."[8] Meeting the practical and immediate needs of those in your community is good. And as we do good because we love people, we win a hearing to provide for their spiritual and eternal need—to tell them about Jesus.

Good works cannot replace the gospel, but they're surely an apologetic for the gospel. David Gustafson put it this way: "Compassionate service provides both a means to demonstrate and an opportunity to tell the gospel."[9] A cup of soup for a homeless guy, or a package of diapers delivered to a struggling new mom, or time taken to teach a refugee how to shop at a grocery store: all show God's love, and all are apologetics for the gospel. Our practical love toward others is a powerful runway from which to deliver the news of God's love.

---

8 Timothy Keller, *Generous Justice: How God's Grace Makes Us Just* (Riverhead Books, 2010), p 142.

9 David M. Gustafson, *Gospel Witness: Evangelism in Word and Deed* (Eerdmans, 2019), p 105.

I'm not saying that good works are only worthwhile if they lead to us sharing the gospel. And I'm not saying we can only share the gospel in conjunction with good works. Evangelism happens in many ways, places, and times. But as we think about being evangelistic churches, good works speak to our corporate witness and reputation in the world. They are not optional extras.

What's Your Reputation?

The people in your neighborhood should be blown away by the love your church has for both insiders and outsiders. The early church was known for this love, and so should we be.

The 4th-century Roman emperor Julian, who was pagan and vehemently opposed to Christianity, "became fearful that Christianity might take over the Roman Empire." Why? "As a result of the good works of Christians."[10] Christians in Rome were supporting thousands of needy people per day. They established hospitals, food programs, and orphanages. Their love for the community was clear and tangible. They were zealous for good works, and it didn't go unnoticed. Julian wrote, "Observe how the kindness of Christians to strangers, their care for the burial of their dead, and the sobriety of their lifestyle has done the most to advance their cause." Even a pagan ruler understood the power of good works done unto Christ.

---

10 As above, p 111.

The sad reality is that many people in our communities are averse to going to church or even talking about Christianity—and often their reticence is because of Christians. Public scandals involving people who claim to be Christians have soured unbelievers toward us. Media outlets and Hollywood often give a poor representation of the church. Social media adds fuel to the fire. We're misrepresented by celebrities and best-selling authors who claim to be for Jesus but are clearly self-focused. And, let's be honest, we ourselves are sometimes guilty of leaving people with a very wrong impression of what Jesus wants his church to be.

This leads to a complete and understandable misunderstanding of the church and of Christianity. That's why it's crucial for local churches to prepare the ground around them—to do good works so that people might be ready to receive the good news. And good works are a commentary on the transforming effects of the true gospel. They can lead those around us to think, "I don't like the 'Christianity' I read about in the newspaper and that I saw in that film and that I experienced from that judgmental person in my past, but I do like what I'm seeing in those people who go to that church near here. That looks different than what I thought Christians were like."

Seventeen centuries after Julian wrote of the power of good works, I saw this happen on the block in Philadelphia.

I was serving at a church in the Kensington section of the city, and we had set up a street clean-up outreach for our neighbors. Early in the day, a lady walked by, looking noticeably sad, troubled, and exhausted. My wife Angel approached her, asking, "Are you okay, ma'am?" She was clearly annoyed and answered (with a profanity added for emphasis), "No!" Angel still engaged her in conversation, seeking to care for her. She asked her if she needed food or water. Her response was telling:

"What do I gotta do to get it?"

I stepped in and told her, "Nothing—it's free."

I explained what we were doing. This angered her further because she realized we were part of a church. She'd been deeply wounded by a church in the past and clearly wanted nothing to do with us. She suggested that we would make her join our church before she could get our help. I made it clear this wasn't the case—that our offering was genuinely free.

She left that conversation with food and clothing. We thought we'd seen the last of her, but after about half an hour she appeared again. Her posture was different this time.

She had come back to thank us.

She told us that a few hours before she walked past us that morning, her father (who lived with her) had stolen all her money and food stamps. She was 22 years old, and she had four hungry kids at home. When she had met us earlier that day, she'd actually been on her way to sell her body for money to feed her kids. Now she would not do so.

We prayed with her and cried with her, offering a tangible expression of the gospel.

Our church helped this young woman and, by God's providence, kept her from trouble that day. I don't know if she ever obeyed the gospel and came to faith, but we did hear around the neighborhood that she'd been talking about us, saying, "They love people who don't even go to their church and aren't Christians." Our help had opened the door for her to hear and experience the good news. This is a key aspect of an evangelistic church—seeking to care for the hurting and recognizing the God-given opportunities to serve its city.

A lady in Philly and a Roman emperor saw the same thing. Good works make an impression. How about your community? What do people living around you think about your church? What does your mayor, police chief, or city council think of your church? Redeem the rumors. Win a hearing for Christ by showing people in what you do what he is like.

A Practical Plan
Here are five practical steps to help prepare your neighborhood for gospel growth.

1. Cultivate Prayerfulness

As we saw in the previous chapter, this is where it starts. Pray corporately and individually for the lost people in your city, and for the Holy Spirit to open their ears to hear the good news. If you skipped chapter 1 on prayer, stop right here and go back and read it!

2. Cultivate the People of God

It isn't enough to encourage the people of your church to do good in the community. They have to understand why their good works are an essential part of evangelism. Without proper biblical preaching, teaching, and training, people will be wandering around with a misplaced sense of purpose. Consider doing a sermon series, class, or seminar looking at the relationship between good works, loving our neighbor, and sharing the gospel. Make these points regular applications in your sermons, classes, or lessons. Make sure people understand that good works and the good news are both mandatory, both for individuals and for the church.

3. Cultivate a Plan

Research your city. Study the people and the culture. Find out what motivates them. Find out what troubles them. Communicate this to your church. Create opportunities for the people of your church to regularly engage with the lost and least in your community. Don't fall into the well-meaning trap of seeing evangelism as an isolated singular event. Mix it in with good works, year round, around the clock. Talk with community leaders, neighbors, and police officers who can give you a sense of the social and spiritual climate of your community. And then talk together as a church, or as a leadership, and plan on how to engage. Consider creating a team in your church that is dedicated to finding the needs in your context and mobilizing the church to meet them.

As you do this, consider collaborating with others. You want to feed the homeless? Partner with your local homeless shelter. Find ways to come alongside the work they're already doing, and seek to be a gospel presence while meeting a tangible need. Want to serve underprivileged kids in your neighborhood? Connect with a local school and get a list of supplies they need. And so on. When you value the work of others, you're making connections and building trust.

Ask: *What are the needs and problems in our community? How can we practically meet these needs? Are there existing ministries or organizations whom we can partner with? How will we seek to make Christ known while doing that?*

4. Get Going... and Be Patient

After praying, learning, observing, brainstorming, and planning—get to work. Good work. Put the diaper drive and delivery for the pregnancy center on the calendar and in the announcements, and make it happen. Recruit the teachers and mentors needed for the free financial class or resumé-building seminar you will host for the community. Do lawn care for older neighbors near your church's building, open a clothes closet for foster and adoption families, minister in prisons... Whatever it is, get going.

And then be patient.

People will be excited about these ventures. Amen! But people will also need to have their expectations adjusted. There is a reason why our Lord used agricultural analogies for the spread of the gospel. Planting, tending, watering, growing fruit, and harvesting take lots of time. Amid the initial excitement, prepare people (including yourself) for the plodding nature of kingdom work.

Leaders, all of this begins with you. Initiative and endurance are the qualities needed here. Be the first to sign up, first to show up, and last to leave. While you cannot neglect the ministry of word and prayer, you can also be like the apostle Paul, who did not need to be told to remember the poor by the apostles in Jerusalem, for it was "the very thing [he] was eager to do" (Galatians 2:10). There was zero doctrinal or internal conflict for Paul between the ministry of the word and the ministries of mercy. Your eagerness for good works should flow from a primary point—your discipleship with Jesus. Don't do it simply because you're a leader. Don't not do it because you're a leader. Your discipleship with Christ, displayed in leadership, is meant to be a pace car for the rest of the congregation. Be an example in your walk.

Let It Shine

You are the salt of the earth. But if the salt should lose its taste, how can it be made salty? It's no longer good for anything but to be thrown out and trampled under people's feet. You are the light of the world. A city situated on a hill cannot be hidden. No one lights a lamp and puts it under a basket, but rather on a lampstand, and it gives light for all who are in the house. In the same way, let your light shine before others, so that they may see your good works and give glory to your Father in heaven. (Matthew 5:13-16)

We have the power and promise of Christ, so why wouldn't we do all we can to ensure the people around us see it clearly too? It's time to let our light shine. Your community needs to see a church shining bright and offering real help to those in need—practical and temporal help, spiritual and eternal help. Truly evangelistic churches are zealous to do good works out of love for people and to win a hearing for the gospel that saves people.

4. TELLING PEOPLE JESUS IS AWESOME

Personal Evangelism

"There is salvation in no one else, for there is no other name under heaven given to people by which we must be saved." (Acts 4:12)

Throughout the Gospels and the beginning of Acts, Jesus gives his followers both future job descriptions and job imperatives. What they're called to do is what they're commanded to do. And Christ's commands were not confined to the apostles. Much more needed to be accomplished than founding churches around the eastern Mediterranean in the 1st century, because the task is to witness to Christ to the ends of the earth (Acts 1:8). There was (and there remains) a lot of gospel work to be done. Christ's command to go forth and tell his gospel is a universal command to all believers.

The "commissions" of Jesus that are found in the Gospels and the beginning of Acts are well-studied. There are a plethora of books, podcasts, conferences, and courses for leaders and pastors. The call to share the gospel isn't complicated, but it is a command—so we have to take it seriously, whether we're leading a church or the most recent convert in that church.

Missional Mode vs. Maintenance Mode

If we are not careful, our churches can turn into a menu of ministry options, with evangelism becoming just another activity in the church vying for attention in the long list of possibilities. Over time, we can unconsciously allow meetings, programs, traditions, and other good things to incrementally move our church from reaching-the-lost mode to reclining mode—from mission to maintenance.

Maybe your church has a wall or display in the foyer of missionaries you are supporting, who are taking the gospel to another country. Hallelujah. We need missionaries to the nations. *And* we need to see that our membership roster is also a missionary roster. Spurgeon was right when he told his church, "Every Christian here is either a missionary or an impostor." What kind of disciples are you making in your church? Is mission fundamental to your functional view of discipleship or is it merely an option for the mature? Does your church see themselves as a group of missionaries called to engage in personal evangelism—and not just the pastors and leaders? When we think about being evangelistic churches, it is vital to focus on prayer, crucial to see how good works fits with the good news, and critical to consider our posture. Yet they would all be for nothing without this chapter. We cannot be evangelistic churches if there is not a culture of every-member personal evangelism.

Two Very Obvious, Much-Forgotten Points

As we start, there are two things we need to clear up about personal evangelism. Both are statements of the obvious. While both these points are obvious to the brain, they are easy to forget in the way we go about our lives and ministries.

1. Personal Evangelism Is Personal

Personal evangelism is not inviting someone to church and letting the pastor preach the gospel. Nor is it preaching for conversions. (You could call that impersonal evangelism.) Posting videos on social media is not personal evangelism. We are talking about *personal* evangelism, when a Christian has a person-to-person interaction about the person and work of Christ and tells someone how they need to respond to the grace and truth of Jesus.

So, when is the last time you shared the gospel with someone? As a church leader, don't let a sermon, a lesson, or a conversation after a service with who was invited to church that day provide you cover from this question. Of course, let's preach and teach the gospel every time we open the Bible—but how are you doing in *personal* evangelism? We know it's more challenging as a church leader. You are surrounded by Christians, work with Christians, and work for Christians. We hope all your coworkers are already saved! As a leader, you will have to work twice as hard to do personal evangelism. But do not ask those you lead to do what you what you are not doing yourself.

2. Personal Evangelism Is Evangelistic

Telling someone that Jesus helped you with a stressful day isn't evangelism. Offering to pray for someone isn't evangelism. Telling people what you did on Sunday or how you serve your church isn't either. Evangelism is more than mentioning Christian-y things. Evangelism is explicit on the *evangel*—the gospel, the news of Jesus' death and resurrection for our sins and the call to repent and believe in him. Spell it out for people. However you explain the gospel (and most of us have our favorite ways to map it out or draw it out), be sure that you make the events of Easter weekend crystal clear. Tell people who Jesus is, what Jesus did, and what they should do in response.

A few months ago, in a rush to board a flight, I (Jeff) stopped at a Starbucks in Terminal E of Houston's massive airport. And to my shock, no one was in line. I said to the barista, "I love this Starbucks. It's almost always empty!" He replied, 'Yeah, man, I like it too. You seem like you're in a good mood. What do you do for work?" I said back, "I help guys start churches all around the world." "Cool, cool," he said. (In my experience, no one knows how to respond to me telling them what I do for a job.) I followed up: "You ever heard of Jesus? Christianity?" He said he'd heard a little bit but didn't really know much. So I explained everything I could about Jesus, sin, and forgiveness as he made my drink. I asked why he thought Jesus would teach about himself being the way, the truth, and the life, and why Jesus would say he is God, and why Jesus would willingly die for sinners. He looked at me intently: "I guess Jesus was serious. He meant it." I told him all he must do is believe, and that God sent me there to tell him the good news. I told him since I fly a lot that I'd be back to see if he'd become a Christian. His name is Javier. I pray for Javier often.

Personal evangelism is a *personal* conversation about the *evangel*. Who is the last person you shared the gospel with? Do you remember their name? Why not pray for them now to come to know Christ before we continue. Please pray for Javier too.

Just Go Tell People How Awesome Jesus Is

The essence of evangelism that we've shared time after time with people is simply this:

Just go tell people how awesome Jesus is.

"Just Go..."

We need to recognize and teach the simplicity of evangelism. This is a simple charge for all believers to share Christ, always and often. To neglect personal evangelism is to disregard the mission of God, to ignore the command of Christ, and to cease being the kind of church that truly follows him:

- In John 20:21, Christ describes the nature of the disciples' calling when he says, "As the Father has sent me, I also send you."

- In Acts 1:8, Christ gives his last exhortations to his apostles, "You will be my witnesses in Jerusalem, in all Judea and Samaria, and to the ends of the earth."

- Most famously, in Matthew 28:19-20, Christ gives what has since been called his Great Commission: "Go, therefore, and make disciples of all nations, baptizing them in the name of the Father and of the Son and of the Holy Spirit, teaching them to observe all that I have commanded you."

We know you probably know those verses. Your church likely knows them too. But they need to be lived, not simply known. This isn't optional for Christians. These are not mere suggestions or helpful tips for ministry leaders; they are God's word and should be revered as such. "Sentness" isn't a spiritual gift, a personality trait, or a work rhythm—it's our calling. We must take it seriously. We are sent, so we go. Is your church leadership paying as much attention to church members living out their calling to evangelism and going-ness as to their giving, small group participation, and service in the church?

"Tell People"

The Bible gives us various glorious identities as believers. Children of God, saints, brothers and sisters of Jesus and of each other, disciples... and witnesses. Every Christian is a witness:

- Luke 24:46–49: "He also said to them, 'This is what is written: The Messiah will suffer and rise from the dead the third day, and repentance for forgiveness of sins will be proclaimed in his name to all the nations, beginning at Jerusalem. You are witnesses of these things. And look, I am sending you what my Father promised. As for you, stay in the city until you are empowered from on high.'"

- Acts 1:8: "But you will receive power when the Holy Spirit has come on you, and you will be my witnesses in Jerusalem, in all Judea and Samaria, and to the ends of the earth."

- Acts 2:32: "God has raised this Jesus; we are all witnesses of this."

- Acts 3:15: "You killed the source of life, whom God raised from the dead; we are witnesses of this." (See also 5:30-32; 10:39-43; 13:29-31.)

- Revelation 2:13: "You hold fast my name, and you did not deny my faith even in the days of Antipas my faithful witness, who was killed among you."

Let's not underbake what it means to be a witness as part of our core identity as Christ's disciples. Witnesses tell people what they saw. Witnesses explain what they experienced. Witnesses inform. Witnesses tell people the truth about what happened. And while we are not eyewitnesses in the way the apostles were, we are witnesses in the way Antipas was in the city of Pergamum. We are not the witnesses who took the gospel of Jesus to Jerusalem, to Judea, or to Samaria. We are those who are taking it to the ends of the earth. While not everyone has the gift of evangelism or considers themselves an evangelist, we are all called to do the work of a witness—to tell people what we have seen of Jesus with the eyes of faith, in the pages of history and in our own lives.

"How Awesome Jesus Is."

People are often nervous about evangelism because they don't want to wade into the culture's hot topics, or they don't feel equipped to engage in apologetic arguments. The apostle Peter helps us reframe the content of our evangelism in 1 Peter 2.

But you are a chosen race, a royal priesthood, a holy nation, a people for his own possession, that you may proclaim the excellencies of him who called you out of darkness into his marvelous light. Once you were not a people, but now you are God's people; once you had not received mercy, but now you have received mercy.

(1 Peter 2:9-10, ESV)

Most of this passage is about who we are, as believers. After framing our identity, Peter sets the activity that flows from that identity—"that you may proclaim." The word "proclaim" here in Greek is only used one time in the whole Bible. The word is *exangéllō*, similar to the word "gospel": *euangélion*. Peter sees Christians as proclaimers, heralds, "make-knowners" of the gospel and the excellencies of Jesus. He says we are to proclaim "the excellencies of him."

In other words, the task and the privilege of every Christian is to simply tell others how awesome Jesus is.

We can tell them how wonderful he is. We can tell them how incredible he is. We don't have to get embroiled in an argument. Proclamation isn't argumentation. We don't have to have every answer. We can say, "I don't know—let me think about that and get back to you. But for the moment, can I tell you why I believe Jesus is the key to life and eternity?" We can think about the ways in which Jesus is amazing—his perfection, sinlessness, deity, kindness, mercy, power, miracles, teaching—and make them known. And most of all, we can talk about how incredible it is that Jesus would die on a Roman cross for sinners like us. We can share how amazing it is that Jesus would die in our place and that he would rise again from the dead and is reigning in heaven, offering real joy-producing, life-altering forgiveness for anyone who believes in him. We can talk about amazing grace, non-expiring mercy, eternal life, and the love of God.

What amazes you about Jesus? What do you love about Jesus? Talk about *that* with people.

And, by the way, talk to your church about how excellent Jesus is. Notice that Peter spends more time in this text exciting Christians about their identity in Christ than he does telling them what to go and do. If Christians are amazed by who they are by faith in Jesus, then they will be far more likely to go and tell others how awesome Jesus is. After all, all of us talk about what we love and what excites us. For some, that's last night's game or the show we went to at the weekend or what our toddler just started to do. For me (Jeff), it's Jeni's ice cream, as I've shared. For us as believers, it's always and supremely Jesus.

Peter does something else here: he connects the personal experience of conversion to our proclamation of Christ's excellencies. "Once you had not received mercy, but now you have received mercy." That is every believer's story. Our personal testimonies of conversion and God's work in our lives can be a part of our proclamation because they are part of his excellencies. This is why we see Paul, who never missed an opportunity to share the gospel, sharing it through telling his own story

(Acts 21:37 – 22:21; 26:1-29). Paul sets out who he was before Jesus intervened, who Jesus is, what Jesus did for him, and the difference Jesus has made to him—and then he asks those he's speaking with what they make of Jesus.

People Really Are Ready to Hear

Evangelism is telling people how awesome Jesus is. And a lot of those people, it turns out, are open to hearing about him. A 2021 study from Lifeway Research of around 1,000 Americans revealed compelling data that speaks to personal evangelism in the United States.

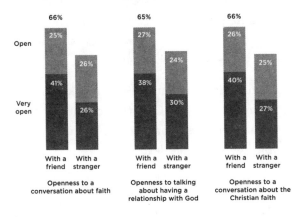

"When meeting someone new," the study also found, "71% say they are open or very open to hearing their life story."[11] 71% of people you meet are willing to hear your life story! A story that we know is all about

---

11 research.lifeway.com/wp-content/uploads/2022/08/Evangelism-Explosion-Survey-of-American-Christians-Report-8_4_22.pdf (accessed March 5, 2024).

the Lord Jesus. Even in the UK, which is considerably more secular and post-Christian than almost anywhere in the US, 75% of non-Christians who had had a conversation with a Christian friend about Jesus said they felt comfortable doing so, and 33% of them left the conversation wanting to know more about Christ. That's one in three! Yet in the same Talking Jesus Survey in 2022, only 55% of the non-Christians who knew a Christian said that that Christian had ever talked to them about their faith in Jesus.[12]

The conclusion: more people are willing to hear our life story than we think. And more people are willing to talk about Christianity than we tend to think. The problem is not that people are rejecting our witness so much as that we are not witnessing in the first place.

Evangelism is simpler than we often make it, and even in our increasingly post-Christian culture, it is better received than we often imagine. We just need to go and tell people how awesome Jesus is.

Three Antidotes to Common Barriers

Wise church leadership will anticipate the struggles and objections people will have as they hear the call to do the work of personal evangelism. We must not allow barriers, whether real or contrived ones, to hinder or halt our evangelism. In my (Doug's) time as a believer,

---

12 https://talkingjesus.org/research (accessed March 5, 2024).

pastor, planter, and professor, I've come across three main barriers to Christians living out a gospel-rooted personal evangelism. I've learned that I need to anticipate those and give an antidote to each.

1. Fear of Rejection

Antidote: "For I consider that the sufferings of this present time are not worth comparing with the glory that is going to be revealed to us" (Romans 8:18). Why would we fear others when we're called to love others and fear God? Our hope and future glory are found in the kingdom, not the culture. That's why we serve the former and not the latter.

Yes, we risk rejection when we share the gospel. In Matthew 10:22 Jesus tells his disciples, "You will be hated by everyone because of my name." The same world that crucified Christ would turn their malice toward his disciples—his witnesses. Outward hostility and rejection shouldn't keep us from proclaiming the name of Christ, because this world is not where our hopes are set and this world is not where we belong. We know there is a glory to be revealed, in eternity. How can we allow rejection in this world to prevent us from inviting those lost in this world to join us in glory?

2. Lack of Bible Knowledge

Antidote: Jesus told us in Matthew 10:18-20, "You will even be brought before governors and kings because of me, to bear witness to them and to the Gentiles. But when they hand you over, don't worry about how or what you are to speak. For you will be given what to say at that hour, because it isn't you speaking, but the Spirit of your Father is speaking through you." Remember our definition of evangelism? It's simple. Just tell people Jesus is amazing! And trust that the Holy Spirit will give you the words, insights, and verses to recall as you witness about Jesus. We need to reassure people that it's okay to not know an answer to someone's question—you can admit you don't know, you can show you respect them by going and finding a good, biblical answer, and you can start another conversation about Jesus with them. Any conversation in which we share the gospel—however haltingly, however unpersuasive we sound to ourselves, however many follow-up questions we cannot answer—is one in which the Spirit will go to work. Let's be reminding our people that we do not need to be experts; we need the Spirit, and we have him.

3. Missional Laziness

Antidote: "Do not lack diligence in zeal; be fervent in the Spirit; serve the Lord" (Romans 12:11). Honestly, isn't it the case that we sometimes don't share the gospel because it's too much effort? But people's lives are at stake. If you love Jesus, why wouldn't you want others to know about him? We're called to go and tell, not sit and wait. There's an urgency to the gospel that can't be missed. We need to continually remind ourselves of this as churches, challenging our default to play safe and be lazy.

It Doesn't Look Spectacular, but It Does Look Like Something

I (Doug) want to share a story of how my wife and I seek to live on mission and personally share the gospel. I hope it encourages you, helps you, and shows you the simple, unspectacular, and supernatural act of evangelism.

I love cookouts, and I have a lot of church sisters who can cook very well. These cookouts are filled with rich discussions, arguments, and plenty of reminiscing. They sometimes end with tears, sometimes with laughter, and sometimes with both. Early in my ministry, I saw that hanging around food was a great place for people to let their hair down and open up about their lives—giving me a great opportunity to share the gospel with unbelievers.

So, in every house we've owned, we have made it our business to make our backyard a place for entertaining. We've always committed to inviting strangers (Christians and non-Christians alike) to our home. We recall many people coming to know Jesus, as well as many people rejecting Jesus, at these cookouts. But my wife and I made a resolution that we would continue sharing the gospel in our home, no matter the result.

One particular time, a Muslim woman and her children came to one of our cookouts a few days after she had come across our church through one of our back-to-school bookbag drives. She discovered that I was the pastor and asked me when was the next bookbag drive. It wasn't till the next year, but I had a few bookbags available so I offered them to her, if she needed them. She asked me if, since I was a Christian pastor, I could still help her children with bookbags even though they were Muslim. "Of course!" I said, and I gave them the bookbags and food from the cookout. She made each of her kids thank me and give me a hug. She was clearly really shocked that a Christian was demonstrating care and generosity toward her Muslim family, just because we were neighbors. My wife and I talked about Jesus with her and prayed for her, and she left.

I saw her a few more times after that. We talked about the grace of God, and she made it a point to thank me every time she saw me. And that was as far as it went. I still pray for her.

I tell you this because personal evangelism does not always end up with a salvation story (sorry if you were waiting for that neat bow at the end of this anecdote). But our interactions should always be seeking to end up with us demonstrating the gospel to others and sharing it with others, fully confident that God is the one who saves.

How to Cultivate Personal Evangelism in Your Church

Okay, you may be thinking, *I want personal evangelism to be part of the culture and expectation of our church. But... how?* Well, we would encourage you and your leadership team to pray and brainstorm ways in which you can develop an evangelistic mindset and heartbeat in your people. But to get things started, here are three things to help foster that kind of culture.

1. Model Evangelism

Share the gospel yourself. Share it with an Uber driver. Share it with the guy who cuts your hair. Share it with your neighbors. Model non-weird, organic, authentic sharing of the excellencies of Christ. Evangelistic churches have evangelistic leaders. If you know you are lagging in evangelism, begin with your own obedience and growth in personally proclaiming the amazingness of Jesus.

2. Mention Evangelism

Share stories of personal evangelism in your sermons. And as with both of our stories in this chapter, don't only mention conversion stories. Share accounts of personal evangelism across the spectrum—times when you were afraid and you were bold, times of praying and proclaiming, times of rejection and times of conversions. Give stage time for testimonies from members who are evangelizing or for someone who wants prayer for an opportunity coming up. Celebrate evangelistic faithfulness in members' meetings or prayer meetings. Interview church members who are already making personal evangelism part of their day-to-day life. Get creative. Get others involved. In what existing spaces could you call attention to evangelism?

3. Mold People for Evangelism

Train your people up. In what ways could you practically encourage and disciple your members in evangelism? Give away books on evangelism to every member. Teach on evangelism in your membership process. Make an evangelism seminar or class a part of the regular rotation of classes and training.

And be patient. Fostering an every-member culture of soul-winning probably won't happen overnight. Don't get frustrated with the church because you did a handful of sermons on evangelism and haven't seen any movement. Gospel fruit takes time. Culture takes time and intentionality to build. It requires months, perhaps years, of ploughing, planting, weeding, watering, pruning, and waiting. Put in the time, the prayers, and the care. Model personal evangelism, mention personal evangelism, and mold people for personal evangelism—and keep on doing it. God is at work.

5. SIX QUESTIONS

Preaching and Teaching
for Conversion

Preaching is personal. Every preacher has their method. You will have your own schedule and habits for reading, meditating on, and studying God's word to proclaim God's word. Our aim in this chapter is not to change your way but to consider how you can, in your way, preach for conversion. Whether you are the main preaching pastor or on a church's teaching team, or you teach students or children, or whatever teaching ministry you're part of, you can translate what you read here to these areas too.

We aren't trying to cover everything about preaching. Much—most—will remain unsaid. There are dozens of books to help you round out and grow in the overall practice of preaching. *Preaching and Preachers* by D. Martyn Lloyd Jones, *The Christ-Centered Expositor* by Tony Merida, *Preaching to a Post-Everything World* by Zack Eswine,

Lectures to My Students by C.H. Spurgeon... all these are masterclasses on preaching. Here, we are offering you a breakout session. We have picked one lane—preaching for conversion—and want to invite you to explore it. We have over 40 years of preaching experience between us, of 40-plus weeks a year and multiple services every Sunday, but we certainly don't see ourselves as finished articles (and you may have more years and more sermons behind you than us). We want to keep growing as sharers of the gospel too. We've learned a lot from friends and mentors over the years, and the case studies in this chapter will provide even more contours and clarity on how to preach for conversion.

Here, we'll simply ask you six questions about your sermons and the overall teaching ministry of your church. They are specific to preaching and teaching the Bible in a soul-winning, conversion-seeking way. We know salvation belongs to the Lord and that the Spirit moves where he wishes. Yet there are also certain ways in which we ought to think, study, and preach in order to raise the sail that can catch the wind of the Spirit as he blows. After all, "how can they believe without hearing about him? And how can they hear without a preacher?" (Romans 10:14).

1. Are We Preaching to the Non-Christians in the Room?

Sermons are for building up the body of Christ—and they are *also* for evangelizing the lost who have found their way to church. This is both-and, not either-or.

You may think you don't have any non-Christians present, but you do. Unless you are confident that every child, teenager, college student, and adult in the congregation is a Christian, there are non-Christians listening. In your preaching, do you ever address the skeptics and unbelievers when appropriate? "You who may not believe in Christ today, and I'm thrilled you are here, consider what God is saying..." "If you are someone who is thinking these things through, here's one claim the Bible makes that is worth pondering..."

Two things happen when you preach to non-Christians. First, your members learn that they can invite their non-Christian friends to any Sunday gathering and they will be seen, spoken to rather than just spoken about, and offered the gospel in a way that they can understand. Second, your members are learning from you how to evangelize. You're doing evangelism and discipleship at the same time.

So be sure to preach in a way that doesn't tangle up the non-Christian. Use plain words as much as possible. Christ's first preachers were uneducated fishermen. They felt no need—and had no ability—to use lofty words. Paul, on the other hand, was an educated man, but he stood against loquacious verbosity because he was for the clear preaching of Christ (1 Corinthians 1:17; 2:4-5).

George Whitefield, the great revival preacher of the American colonies, was known for purposefully using "market language"—the speech and style of everyday people. Are your sermons filled with stuffy jargon and unexplained or underexplained theological terms? Aseity, forensic justification, incommunicable? Are you explaining words that Christians tend to use differently than secular culture does—words like economy, redeem, repent, sin? We need to patiently, creatively, and clearly explain complex concepts in simple, relatable, and relevant language. Illustrate with word pictures, real-world examples, and familiar stories that point to the gospel story. It's what Jesus did.

2. Are We Preaching Christ Every Week?

To preach for conversion means you relentlessly preach Christ. As Charles Spurgeon said in his book *The Soul-Winner*, "I believe that those sermons which are fullest of Christ are the most likely to be blessed to the conversion of the hearers. Let your sermons be full of Christ, from beginning to end crammed full of the gospel."[13] Is Jesus the obvious subject of your sermon? This doesn't mean that our sermons are only about Jesus. It means that he is the Noun of nouns in our sermons. Look at your most recent manuscript or outline—is it crammed with Jesus or does he only make a cameo appearance? May we never preach a Jesus-less sermon. That's Satan's favorite kind.

---

13 C.H. Spurgeon, *The Soul Winner: How to Lead Sinners to the Saviour* (Fleming H. Revell, 1895), p 99.

If you want to bring sinners to Christ, bring Christ to sinners. Preach and teach everything in relation to him who is Lord of all. As Tim Keller wrote:

Every time you expound a Bible text you are not finished unless you demonstrate how it shows us that we cannot save ourselves and that only Jesus can. That means we must preach Christ from every text, which is the same as saying we must preach the gospel every time and not just settle for general inspiration or moralizing.[14]

Think about Paul's resolution: "I decided to know nothing among you except Jesus Christ and him crucified" (1 Corinthians 2:2). He made up his mind to make Jesus the radiating core of his ministry. 1 Corinthians touches on almost every subject in the Christian life, but, while Paul talked about more than the gospel, he never did less than talk about the gospel, and he taught everything in light of the gospel. Jesus was always his subject: "We proclaim him, warning and teaching everyone with all wisdom, so that we may present everyone mature in Christ" (Colossians 1:28).

We should always allow the passage at hand to guide us toward Christ. No shoehorning of the Savior into the text is needed. Jesus is the true north of the text. We only need to give the text time in our study and prayers

---

14 Timothy Keller, *Preaching: Communicating Faith in an Age of Skepticism* (Viking, 2015), p 48.

to point us to him. I (Jeff) have found a framework of four Ms that helps ensure that my sermons are crammed full of Christ, while also not formulaic in what I say about Christ. Not all four of these Ms might be present in the text or sermon, but at least one will arise organically from the passage:

1. Jesus is the message.

2. Jesus is the motivation.

3. Jesus is the model.

4. Jesus is the means.

Jesus as the *message* points to how he is our Savior, our Lord, and the ultimate hero of every passage, narrative, book, and genre of the Bible. Everything and everyone in the Bible points to Jesus. And from this reality, we tell unbelievers that he is who they need: straightforward gospel proclamation and invitation. A text on love will lead us to God's love made incarnate. A passage on holiness ought to eventually usher us to the holy one. And so on.

Jesus is the ultimate *motivation* for good works, holiness, and loving others. This is vital for true Christian spirituality. Christians live for Christ because "he died for all so that those who live should no longer live for themselves, but for the one who died for them and was raised" (2 Corinthians 5:15). And we connect this point to unbelievers by asking them to think about why they do what they do. We show them the difference that living life for Christ, with him as their ruler, would make to them, and the difference it would make through them to those around them. Life lived with and for Christ is *better*.

Jesus as the *model* must be threaded carefully. We should never give the impression that Jesus is merely an aspirational and inspirational Messiah; he is a transformational one. But nevertheless, we can't underemphasize that being Christ's disciple means seeking to become like him—to follow his example (Luke 6:40; Romans 8:29). Christ's love for the church is the model of marriage (Ephesians 5:25). Christians forgive in the way that God has forgiven us in Christ (Ephesians 4:32). Jesus shows us what life looks like. We can show non-Christians that there is a better way to live, a Jesus-like way, the way we were designed to walk through life—and from here we tell unbelievers that not only can Christ be their model but that he must also be their Lord, setting the agenda for their lives, and their Savior, forgiving them for their ongoing inability to live as they should. And this brings us back to Jesus as the message for forgiveness and new life in him, through him, and for him.

Lastly, we preach Jesus as the *means*—the engine, fuel, muscle—of the Christian life. We locate the root of our obedience, evangelism, repentance—everything!—in the crucified and risen Christ, who said that apart from him we can do nothing (John 15:5) and who sent his

Spirit to empower our obedience. He is the only way to eternal life, forgiveness, shame being removed, condemnation being lifted, and us resting in the love of God and being transformed into the people we long to be and that he calls us to be. Jesus does not just show us who to be and forgive us when we fail—he enables us to become what we're called to be. We can tell non-Christians to give up their efforts to make life work or to find forgiveness in their own strength. We can offer them Christ, the Savior and sustainer of forgiven sinners.

3. Are We Preaching *All* of Christ's Person and Work?

Evangelistic churches preach evangelistic sermons. Their sermons are not merely evangelistic, without meat for Christians. But they *are* always evangelistic.

This means preaching Jesus as incarnate, as the God-Man. It means the old-school message of Christ crucified as our substitute, lifting him up for all to look upon by preaching his bloody cross.

But not only the cross.

I'm convinced that the second half of Easter weekend is the most neglected truth in evangelical church sermons today.

The cross of Jesus is not the end of the good news. Rome crucified many people; but only Jesus's brainstem turned back on three days later. Jesus is alive and well. I know we know that—but is Jesus alive in our sermons? We are truly preaching the full, historic, supernatural gospel when we proclaim that Christ died and yet he lives. People should walk out of churches thinking, "This church really believes that Jesus is alive right now, that he is doing things right now." We get to preach the living Christ to dead sinners! And it's the living Jesus who wants to make sinners alive in him.

Let's keep proclaiming the cross of Christ—yes and amen!—but what about his resurrection? We must sound both notes. Christ rising is more than a divine announcement that the cross worked. It is part of our salvation because Christ was "raised for our justification" (Romans 4:25). Let's raise the resurrection to be on a par with the cross in our preaching.

"If Christ has not been raised, then our proclamation is in vain, and so is your faith … And if Christ has not been raised, your faith is worthless; you are still in your sins" (1 Corinthians 15:14, 17). If there is no resurrection with Christ as the firstborn from the dead, then we have nothing to offer sinners because Christ has nothing to offer us. But since he lives, everything is different, possible, and promised. The risen Christ is our living hope, the kind of hope saints, sinners, and sufferers need. The gospel-centered movement has helped us avoid teaching like legalistic and graceless Pharisees. But are we starting to sound like the Sadducees, who didn't preach a resurrection of the dead? We need to preach the risen Christ every single Sunday rather than just on Easter Sunday. No one needs a still-dead Jesus. So get Jesus on the cross, in the grave, out of the tomb, and at the Father's right hand—and let everyone know why this is the good news. His risen body is why there is hope. We live in the atmosphere of the Lord Jesus Christ's resurrection. Make it plain that he lives and breathes.

4. Do Our Sermons Call for a Response?

If the resurrection of Jesus is the most underplayed aspect of the gospel message, then perhaps the runner-up in that competition would be another r: repentance.

The Gospels describe the content of our Lord's word ministry as "proclaiming the good news of God: 'The time is fulfilled, and the kingdom of God has come near. Repent and believe the good news!'" (Mark 1:14–15; see also Matthew 4:17). Jesus made it clear that he came to call "sinners to repentance" (Luke 5:32). And when he commissioned his disciples to go out in groups of two, they "went out and preached that people should repent" (Mark 6:12). It was "repentance for the forgiveness of sins" that Jesus tasked his followers with preaching in his name to all nations (Luke 24:47). Peter did that at Pentecost (Acts 2:38) and in Solomon's Portico (3:19) and again when on trial before the Sanhedrin (5:31). Paul preached that, "God now commands all people everywhere to repent, because he has set a day when he is going to judge the world in righteousness by the man he has appointed. He has provided proof of this to everyone by raising him from the dead" (17:30).

Our sermons should regularly remind Christians to confess and repent of any sins as part of their ongoing sanctification. And soul-winning sermons also call non-Christians to an initial "foundation of repentance" (Hebrews 6:1): a repentance from sin—not just sins—and a turn to Christ.

I'm not arguing for a boilerplate paragraph about repentance that you drop into each sermon. Instead, as we work through a passage, there are certain launch words and themes that can preach the command and invitation of repentance and faith in Christ. These are elements that can create a moment to address the non-Christians, words that can personally introduce your hearers to the living Jesus—words like "whoever" or "anyone" or "all people." Spurgeon would even use the word "look" as an avenue through which to invite unbelievers to look to Jesus. *Anyone can look. A child can look. It takes no special pedigree or moral standing to look.* When I come across these words, I aim to open them as the invitation they are for sinners to come to Jesus. To give one example, when I preached at a difficult funeral and saw the word "whoever" in Psalm 91:1—"Whoever dwells in the shelter of the Most High will rest in the shadow of the Almighty" (NIV)—I found my angle. I said:

"Whoever." Isn't that a beautiful word? It's a word of grace. It's an inviting word. Listen to me: you are

a "whoever." The Scripture doesn't say, "Only if you grew up in church. Or if you haven't done this sin or that sin. Or only if your read the Bible, pray, and on and on." No, that's not how Jesus operates. Jesus went to the cross for all kinds of people. Every kind of sinner. He went for "whoevers." And Jesus is alive right now, speaking from this word "whoever," and he is saying, "Whoever wants my forgiveness, my life, my standing before God—whoever wants me—I will save." He is alive and ready to save. No matter how big your sin, how deep a hole you are in, how much shame you feel—the one who overcame death is extending his hand to whoever wants it.

Preaching for conversion, as in the Gospels and Acts, means we will preach repentance and faith in Christ.

5. Are We Considering Backgrounds and Barriers?

If you are preaching in a context that is well-versed in the Scriptures—a Bible-belt or a religious area—you might sound like Peter in Acts 2. To lay out the life, death, and resurrection of Jesus and the necessary response of repentance and faith, Peter talked about the prophetic expectation of the Messiah, he spoke about King David, and he quoted the Psalms. His audience was well versed in the Old Testament, and so his words struck home (v 37).

If you are in an area where most people think they are Christians—even the people who are only members of

Bedside Baptist or First Mattress Church—the temptation is to assume that everyone is indeed a Christian.

I grew up in such a setting, attending a healthy, gospel-heralding Southern Baptist church. On one typical Sunday evening, the pastor was preaching Christ and inviting people to receive Christ and to indicate their desire to repent and believe by walking forward.

My mother went forward.

My dad, sister, and I all looked at each other. *What's going on?* Mom became a Christian in that sermon—but prior to that, she thought she already was one, and so did we. Yet it was the preaching of the gospel that day that brought her to actual saving trust in Jesus. If you are in a "churched" context, there are multiple generations of people who need to hear evangelistic sermons and meet the risen Christ for real. Many people need to be converted from their idea of Christianity and be converted to Christ.

If you are in a more secular context where people have little or no knowledge of the Bible, let Paul in Acts 17 be your guide. Paul started by noticing Athenian culture and mentioning their spirituality, and then moved on to proclaim God as Creator before arriving at the resurrection of Jesus. Paul did not speak down to people gathered at Mars Hill. He noted how they were "extremely religious in every respect" (Acts 17:22). Paul didn't crack his homiletical knuckles and offend his hearers. The gospel is offensive enough, and it will offend in its own time and on its own terms. Sermons that pick fights are not sermons preached for conversions. A sermon could win a fight but not win a soul. Look for ways to connect with the values, themes, and desires of your hearers and then show Jesus as the way. Paul saw a cultural connection to the gospel when he noticed an altar with the inscription "To an Unknown God." From there, he gave his listeners a more zoomed-out message about God, false gods, and creation, and then brought it to the risen Jesus and the call to repent.

The point is know your culture, know your setting, and start where people are at. The less background people have with the Scriptures, the more building we need to do. Every Sunday at Houston Northwest Church, Pastor Steve Bezner begins his sermon with a quick overview of the Bible for those who are new. It takes a minute or two. "The Bible is divided up into two parts: the Old and New Testament," he says. "The Old Testament is the story of God's people, Israel, and the promise God made to them of a Messiah: the one who would save them, deliver them, and lead them. The New Testament is about how Jesus of Nazareth is that Messiah, how he died for our sins and rose again from the dead, and how anyone can believe in him, be saved by him, and learn to live with him in what is called the kingdom of God." Steve knows that a complete lack of understanding of the Bible's grand story is a barrier. He breaks it down. It's worth asking what it would look like in your particular setting to locate the barriers and pull them down.

Whether it is the Bible's teaching on marriage or the hypocrisy your hearers observe in the evangelical world, be prepared to provide thoughtful answers to doubts and disagreements in a sermon. Be attuned to what's swirling in the secular culture. But at the same time, Tim Keller showed us one way to address the roadblocks people raise by always bringing Jesus into the conversation. Acknowledge the barrier and help people see what really matters: *You may not like the Bible's teaching on gender— but does that mean Jesus couldn't have died and rose again? Does your personal disagreement with this teaching delete the historical fact of Christ's death and resurrection? If Jesus didn't rise from the dead, then nothing he said matters. But if he did, then everything matters.*

Different contexts will need different launching points and need to take account of different barriers, but the destination is the same: Jesus.

6. Are We Preaching with Urgency and Authenticity?

How do you view yourself as a preacher? I want to offer you a subtle but possibly seismic shift in your identity as a preacher. It will affect the way you pray, study, and preach. Rather than thinking of yourself as just a "preacher" or an "exegete" or even an "expositor," view yourself as a preacher of *Christ*. See yourself as a proclaimer of *Jesus*. Call and view yourself as a herald of *the gospel*.

I am in no way suggesting a lessening of study or preaching sermons that neglect Bible literacy and fidelity. Exegete and exposit till your eyes get crossed on the cross. But if you begin to think of your vocation as a proclaimer of Jesus, it will set the course of your heart, your study, your prayers, and your sermons. The undercurrent of your sermon prep and writing becomes "I *must* make Christ known to my hearers." The *who* we are sets the trajectory for *what* we do.

And it sets the tone for *how* we do it.

We will preach Christ passionately, urgently, and lovingly when we are abiding in, enjoying, and loving Jesus. Christ must be real to us if we are to make him real to others. Francis Grimké captured this when he said, "The very thought of him ought to kindle within our hearts a flame of sacred love, and lead us enthusiastically to put ourselves at his service."[15] There is a kind of preaching in which our personal enjoyment and adoration of Jesus spills out in the public exposition as exultation and exaltation of Jesus. Are you enjoying Jesus? Are you excited about Jesus? When you are, you are itching to talk of Jesus.

Of course every preacher of Christ has their own range of emotions, energy, and expressiveness. We preach as ourselves, not as someone else. But consider what Spurgeon meant when he said:

---

15 Carter G. Woodson (Ed.), *The Works of Francis J. Grimké*, Vol. 3 (Associated Publishers, 1942), p 469.

Among the important elements in the promotion of conversion are your own tone, temper, and spirit in preaching. If you preach the truth in a dull, monotonous style, God may bless it, but in all probability he will not; at any rate the tendency of such a style is not to promote attention, but to hinder it. It is not often that sinners are awakened by ministers who are themselves asleep.[16]

I'll reframe it this way—feel what you are preaching. Be awakened in your soul, mind, body and speech to the glorious good news of grace. Preach like you have *news* that is *good*, news that dying men and women *need* to hear. Preach like everyone, from the pulpit to the parking lot, needs Jesus. Preach as someone who needed conversion to Christ, who has experienced conversion because of Christ, and who is inviting others to receive Christ.

The Problem with Breakouts

I've attended many brilliant breakout sessions. At least I thought they were brilliant while I was sitting in them. As soon as I walked out of the session and headed to either the bookstore or coffee with a friend, I left behind the thoughts I'd had and the plans I'd made about things I wanted to change. What seemed so urgent and implementable in the room became absent and forgettable. Don't copy and paste my conference blunder

---

16 C.H. Spurgeon, "On Conversion As Our Aim," in *Lectures to My Students: Addresses Delivered to the Students of the Pastors' College*, Vol. 2 (Robert Carter and Brothers, 1889), p 277.

when it comes to this chapter. Take some time to review any highlights and underlines you've made. Write down the questions of this chapter and answer them honestly in a journal. Bring the questions to your fellow pastors, teaching team, or elders, and begin a conversation on areas of strength and growth in terms of preaching for conversion. What it would look like to start a sermon review team that considered how the sermon was dialed for preaching for conversion? Maybe put the questions from this chapter on a sticky note on your desk.

Here's a final encouragement—expect conversions. In a sermon titled "Soul Winning," Spurgeon made a helpful point on preaching for conversion: expect God to do it. The pastor who sees conversions, he said, is the one "who expects conversion every time he preaches. According to his faith so shall it be done unto him. To be content without conversions is the surest way never to have them: to drive with a single aim entirely at the saving of souls is the surest method of usefulness. If we sigh and cry till men are saved, saved they will be."[17]

The actually evangelistic church preaches and teaches evangelistically—and it preaches expectantly and excitedly, for God loves to use his heralds to bring men and women to faith.

---

17 C.H. Spurgeon, "Soul Winning," in *The Metropolitan Tabernacle Pulpit*, Vol. 15 (Passmore & Alabaster, 1869), p 32.

6. THE BEGINNING, NOT THE END

A Process for New Converts

Conversion is not the end of our journey with those we've evangelized—in some ways, it's the beginning. The work isn't completed when someone believes.

Even as we become soul-winning churches and foster a culture of evangelism, we need to keep our sights on the full call of Jesus in Matthew 28. He doesn't tell us to make converts or call for decisions. He says, "Make disciples." Churches become disobedient to Christ's commission if we lead people to Christ and yet never show them how to walk with him. Of course, there are times and places where we are unable to follow up, but that's not what we are talking about in this chapter. We want to see churches that tend to the fruit of their evangelism by heeding Christ's call to make disciples.

In this final chapter, we want to help you think strategically about discipling new converts in your church. As Jesus brings people to know him, consider your church's plan and process to develop new disciples in the faith because they're entering as "little children" and "babies in Christ" (1 John 2:12; Hebrews 5:13; 1 Corinthians 3:1-2). New believers need a pathway and framework for growth.

Milk First, Then Meat

Hebrews 5:12 – 6:2 is a passage that addresses the maturity and growth of believers in the Christian faith and emphasizes the need for gospel growth:

> *Although by this time you ought to be teachers, you need someone to teach you the basic principles of God's revelation again. You need milk, not solid food. Now everyone who lives on milk is inexperienced with the message about righteousness, because he is an infant. But solid food is for the mature—for those whose senses have been trained to distinguish between good and evil. Therefore, let us leave the elementary teaching about Christ and go on to maturity, not laying again a foundation of repentance from dead works, faith in God, teaching about ritual washings, laying on of hands, the resurrection of the dead, and eternal judgment.*

Our churches are to be places that disciple people from spiritual infancy toward spiritual maturity. In the church that the author of Hebrews is writing to, it's not happening. When I (Jeff) smoke a brisket, it always hits a stall, when the temperature hits the brakes and the brisket-cooking slows. Barbecue pros say you can wrap the brisket and push past the stall faster. The writer to the Hebrews would not have known much about Texan barbecue, but he speaks to a spiritual stall, and as he does so, he also diagnoses some of the current problems in churches across the evangelical landscape.

The author is straight-up rebuking his letter's recipients for their spiritual immaturity. In colloquial terms, we can hear a mother telling her 21-year-old son, "Boy, it's time to grow up and act your age," after he has done something that you might expect of an 8-year-old. The people the author is challenging about spiritual immaturity have been believing members of the church for some time, but they have not spiritually grown up—they have not achieved the expected progress in their understanding of the Christian faith. So the author utilizes a metaphor about milk and solid food to make his point. The milk is representative of basic, foundational Christian doctrine and practice. And the solid food represents deeper, more complex spiritual truths. These believers should have matured beyond the basic teachings of the faith, and they should now be able to teach others—yet they still need someone to spoon-feed them milk, the fundamentals of the Christian faith.

The point is that stalls in growth will happen if we aren't watching. Our churches must be committed to maturity in the faith through constant learning, discernment, and a commitment to advancing in one's sanctification. But in our time of serving churches, both plants and established ones, we have noticed many churches have a gap in their discipleship pathway. Many don't have an accessible and relational environment for new converts, for the newborns in Christ. Hebrews 5 prompts us to ask: is our church creating stalls in the growth of new believers?

We need to notice two assumptions that the author of Hebrews makes:

1. A church will give foundational spiritual milk to new believers.

2. A church will subsequently wean them onto solid food of God's deeper understanding of the faith.

This guards against two mistakes. The first is starting straight away with the meat, wrongly expecting new converts, babes in Christ, to digest it when what they need is milk. We must start with milk as we seek to see new converts grow from spiritual infancy to spiritual maturity in Christ. Second, it guards us against never moving on to meat, and raising Christians who remain stalled on milk.

It's a Growth Process

Babies need their parents and caregivers every step of the way. They depend on someone else for food, comfort, and cleaning. They can't make their own bottles or change their own diapers. They're autonomous people, made in the image of God, yet they can't help themselves do much of anything at first. This isn't a weakness; it's just a process. As children grow, they gain some independence and responsibility. The same is true for new believers. As they grow in the context of the local church, they should be guided by faithful saints who are spiritually mature.

If a baby has a dirty diaper and is crying in her crib, ignoring her will not help. It will actually make matters worse. Her cries will grow louder and louder until someone attends to her. This isn't because she's annoying or behaving badly; it's just all she knows. There's a problem in her life (a dirty diaper), and she needs it fixed. She does not know how to fix it, but she knows someone who does, and so she cries for them and anticipates that they'll come to help. What does the faithful, loving parent do? They care for their kids and come to their aid. Spiritual mothers and fathers do the same for those we're discipling, emulating our heavenly Father, who cares for us more than we'll ever understand. New converts are going to make messes, too, and we must be "patient with everyone" (1 Thessalonians 5:14). As new converts navigate their first days, weeks, and months as Christians, they'll struggle. You know this because, no matter how seasoned a Christian you are, you still struggle too. God cares for us as we grow—he is a faithful Father, slow to anger and rich in love. He exhorts us to do the same for the spiritual infants among us.

New Christians, like newborns, are time-consuming, exhausting, and just downright hard work—and they are thrilling, rewarding, and glorifying to God. When new converts in your church still act and speak in ways which they did prior to conversion, don't be surprised. A church has to exercise gospel-minded patience with new believers. People come to know Jesus as Savior at varying levels of knowledge and understanding about the faith. The church cannot expect new believers to instantly morph into mature Christians. Every doctrine, command, act of repentance, and transformation is new to new believers.

Just as it takes a child many years to grow into maturity and responsibility, it takes new "babes in Christ" some time to grow too. Don't neglect them. Disciple them patiently, with milk, but with a view to them reaching the time when they will be able to eat meat. And disciple them differently, taking account of their newness to faith. Simply put, in the Christian church, those who are more mature in the faith are to teach those new in the faith how to live a healthy and stable Christian lifestyle in a chaotic, spiritually dangerous world.

Dangers Ahead

In Ephesians 4:12-16 Paul is writing to the entire church community, casting a vision for them to participate in nurturing each other and spurring one another on in their spiritual growth—to do...

the work of ministry, to build up the body of Christ, until we all reach unity in the faith and in the knowledge of God's Son, growing into maturity with a stature measured by Christ's fullness. Then we will no longer be little children, tossed by the waves and blown around by every wind of teaching, by human cunning with cleverness in the techniques of deceit. But speaking the truth in love, let us grow in every way into him who is the head—Christ. From him the whole body, fitted and knit together by every supporting ligament, promotes the growth of the body for building itself up in love by the proper working of each individual part.

The metaphor is of little kids who, due to their lack of strength, are overcome by the winds of a turbulent storm as they stand on a boat and, as a result, are tossed around, thrown down, and injured by the storm. The more someone grows into maturity by becoming more like Christ, the less tossed around they will be by false teaching. New believers lack the spiritual maturity to discern deceitful doctrines and harmful teachings.

New believers are often at the frontlines of facing scoffers, false teachings, and persecution. Unbelieving friends and family may roll their eyes, mock them, or distance themselves from them as they worship a man from Galilee who rose from the dead. In our social-media age, excited new believers may unintentionally end up down a rabbit hole of false teaching without realizing it. The church, and especially leaders of the church, are to help one another be grounded in the truth and to discern false teachings. How will you help new believers learn and understand God's design for church, marriage and singleness, gender, sexuality, finances, careers, children, and so on? The secular culture is constantly discipling the world in its ways, and a gospel culture needs to be intentionally, thoughtfully, zealously discipling followers of Christ in Christ's ways.

The church as a whole is called to protect all its members, especially new believers, from being misled by false teachings and to spur them on to spiritual maturity in the faith.

Growing in Community

As Paul has shown, the best place for new believers to grow in grace is with the people of God. The local church is the ecosystem for spiritual growth. Gospel growth happens within the loving walls of the gospel community. In Christ, a person's past behavior and sin no longer define them, and our churches should reflect the same kind of generosity and full acceptance as our Savior. The world can be a lonely place, and the church is to be a belonging place.

Acts 2 gives a great example of what should happen among God's people when conversions occur. The chapter begins with Pentecost and the coming of the

Holy Spirit to work among Christ's followers after his ascension to heaven. Then, in verses 14-41, Peter preaches the first Spirit-filled sermon, and "about three thousand people" were saved and were baptized (v 41). What an incredible work of the Holy Spirit, to see 3,000 people come to know Jesus! But the story doesn't end there. "They devoted themselves to the apostles' teaching, to the fellowship, to the breaking of bread, and to prayer" (v 42). The new birth of these men and women initiated their growth process. They had "all things in common" and cared for each other by selling their possessions and distributing the wealth to those who needed it. Here is a gospel-rooted, gospel-learning church community.

This underlines two aspects of how we make disciples, teaching them to observe everything Christ has commanded—community and education.

As we've seen already, while God may have used a sermon or a believer's explanation of the gospel to bring about new birth, he intends that a newborn Christian be raised by a family—the local church.

This is what Paul is speaking of in Titus 2:

> *Older men are to be self-controlled, worthy of respect, sensible, and sound in faith, love, and endurance. In the same way, older women are to be reverent in behavior, not slanderers, not slaves to excessive drinking. They are to teach what is good,*

so that they may encourage the young women to
love their husbands and to love their children, to be
self-controlled, pure, workers at home, kind, and in
submission to their husbands, so that God's word
will not be slandered. In the same way, encourage the
young men to be self-controlled in everything. Make
yourself an example of good works with integrity and
dignity in your teaching. (v 2-7)

Gregory of Nyssa, a 4th-century Church Father in Cappadocia (modern-day Turkey), taught that the local church is like a community of wet-nurses—women who nursed and took care of babies born to another woman. Wet-nurses were common in the early centuries because maternal mortality in childbirth was so high. And like Paul, who described himself as a nursing mother among the Thessalonians (1 Thessalonians 2:7), Gregory envisioned this spiritual feeding ministry as a regular ministry throughout the body of Christ. He saw the church as a veritable nursery of discipleship. But how many of our churches are almost solely dependent on the pastor? Sermons are vital to discipleship. Every Christian needs the preaching of the word. We cannot minimize the importance of the pulpit. But no Christian—new or old—can grow on a single meal a week. Christians need to meal-prep for one another: to be ready and "able to instruct one another" (Romans 15:14).

We need to foster a culture where it is understood that church staff and pastors are not the only ones responsible for discipleship. Everyone has a ministry with the word. Everyone is called to informally, relationally "let the word of Christ dwell richly among you, in all wisdom teaching and admonishing one another through psalms, hymns, and spiritual songs, singing to God with gratitude in your hearts" (Colossians 3:16).

Younger believers need to see mature faith lived out in older men and women (older in years or in years in the faith). And they need to hear mature faith spoken about by those older men and women, who "teach what is good" to those coming up behind them (Titus 2:3). The whole community raises a whole Christian. Biblical Christianity sees the entire local church, and not just pastors and leaders, as helping one another to grow in Christ. We all need faithful parents, friends, brothers, sisters, and spiritual mentors. Are you acting as a father or mother in the faith, as a big brother or sister to others, inviting young Christians and especially new or struggling Christians to learn from you, to see faith lived out, to hear faith spoken about? And are you encouraging and envisioning older saints to do the same?

Education and Formation

Those Pentecost converts were not only deeply integrated into the church community; they were also devoted to the apostles' teaching. What does church membership look like for new converts in your church?

The early church developed a process of training, baptizing, and welcoming new converts into the community. They utilized catechisms: a question-and-answer tool to teach Christian doctrine. Andy Burggraff speaks to this in an article entitled *How Did the Early Church Disciple New Believers?*:

> *The early church formulated a method of education (discipleship) for believers to train them in the knowledge and defense of their faith. Much of this training was required before the believer's baptism and, subsequently, membership into the church. Through this process, commitment to Christ was evaluated, discipleship was implemented, education in theology and apologetics was taught, and moral character was mentored and enhanced.*[18]

The late J.I. Packer was a strong proponent of catechesis:

> *Catechesis is both a very biblical idea and a faithful practice of the church through the ages. Where wise catechesis has flourished, the church has flourished. Where it has been neglected, the church has floundered. We catechize in obedience to the Great Commission of our Lord Jesus Christ and in imitation of the Lord's own ministry when he walked among us. He has charged the church to make disciples from all people groups of the earth. This discipling requires a rigorous ministry of*

---

18 shepherds.edu/how-did-the-early-church-disciple-new-believers/ (accessed March 5, 2024).

teaching obedience to all Jesus commanded. Catechesis is precisely such a ministry.[19]

What could this look like for you? Your church could use one of the many catechisms available. You could create a curriculum of essential Christian doctrines and practices for new believers taught either in a classroom setting or through conversations over a year or two. You can scale this to the number of new believers and set up various entry points during the year. Some churches may be able to host a yearly class, while other churches can mobilize mature Christians who will take new converts under their wing on their own schedule. Your church may even be able to launch a Bible Institute or training program like our friend J.T. English writes about in his book *Deep Discipleship*. Some churches may be able to hire a staff member or recruit a volunteer to develop and lead the curriculum, class time, online community, required reading, papers to be written, grading, and even a graduation. Of course these things will depend on the size of your church and the number of mature believers you can look to to help share the teaching burden. Each church's plan will look different and be honed over time. But make sure yours looks like something, and don't be afraid to raise the bar.

New converts need to be taught about their new *life* in Christ. Everything is new to them. New converts could

---

19 J.I. Packer and Gary Parrett, *Grounded in the Gospel: Building Believers the Old-Fashioned Way* (Baker Books, 2010), p 184.

benefit from a kind of orientation meeting with pastors: "Welcome to Christ. Here's what this all means." Teach them how to read the Bible, how to pray, why we take the Lord's Supper, why we sing praises... and how to share the gospel. New converts are new missionaries!

Theological information is for spiritual transformation. Make a disipleship plan for new Christians that covers foundations, essentials, and spiritual disciplines. Get the compass pointed north. If you would like a jumpstart, check the appendix of suggested topics to cover with new converts on page 161.

Celebration and Discipleship

Don't forget: new converts should be celebrated! Let's lead our churches in rejoicing over God's grace! But while we rejoice over newborn Christians, let's not forget our call to disciple them. We need to welcome them, teach them, and show them what growing, living, vibrant, stable faith looks like—on a Sunday and through the week. We're all members of one body and have different but essential roles (Ephesians 4:4-13)—and they are now a vital part of the body of Christ. We evangelize and disciple together. We grow and pray together. We grieve and rejoice together. God made us for community, and he is glorified when we live in relationship with one another. God wants new believers to grow in love for Christ, and he wants your church to help them. And, as you do, you'll find he's growing you in love for him and his people too.

CONCLUSION

In a sense, every book on your bookshelf tells a story. There are the ones that were never opened or were started but nowhere near finished. They tell you a story of what didn't really matter that much or what wasn't really that useful. There are the books which were started and finished, highlighted and scribbled on, and then put on the shelf and quietly forgotten. Perhaps they tell a story of good intentions or of missed opportunities, or of both.

And then there are the books that made a difference. Their spines alone, when you spot them, remind you of the stories of how something significant changed—because the content of those books came to life in your life.

What story will this book tell?

We hope it will tell of a church that changed the way it prayed for the conversion of the lost—that changed the way it thought about witnessing and the way it reached out and the way it shared Christ. We hope it will tell of a church that saw a wave of people coming to faith and being welcomed into the membership and life of the church. We hope that one day, as a younger friend catches sight of the spine of this book on your bookshelf and asks you about it, you can tell them, "By God's grace, that book sparked a season that changed our church."

Books tell a story. And now this part of the story is partly up to you. What will you and your church do? What will you double down on? What will you think about? What will you change? What will you pray?

Where You Are and Where You're Heading

We hope you found in these pages a simple and supernatural plan that any congregation can implement. To help you do just that, here's an evaluation well worth doing before this book is introduced to your bookshelf. Honest evaluations are a part of any growth or change process. Thermometers, x-rays, and stopwatches are evaluators. They have no agendas—they just give readings. Let the axis opposite serve as a reading on the evangelistic temperature of your church's culture. If you are reading with a group from your church, do an evaluation together. How do you "read" your church and your church's leadership when it comes to our six Ps of a genuinely evangelistic church?

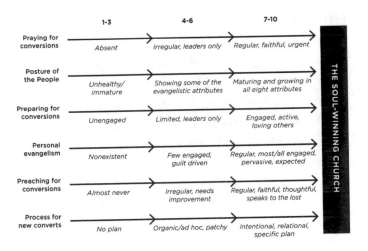

Discuss the results. (If your scores differ, that in itself is an area for fruitful conversation.) This is where you are right now, as a church.

What encouragements are there, which you can share widely?

Where do you want to get to: In a year? In five years? Eventually?

What positive steps will you take to start moving your church further to the right-hand end of these lines?

In other words, what do you dream the future history of your church will be? You can begin today. You can start a wise, patient yet fervent process toward becoming a soul-winning church.

Lift Him Up

When we obey God—when we do God's work in God's way—God's results are the outcome. Jesus says, "As for me, if I am lifted up from the earth I will draw all people to myself" (John 12:32). We hope the pages of this book aid and inspire each person and congregation to lift Jesus high in their lives and actions and words—on Sundays and every other day. Because, having been lifted up in his death and resurrection and ascension, and as he is lifted up by our witness to him, Jesus promises to draw people to himself. We pray, and he answers. We speak, and he saves. We preach, and he draws. Let Jesus' gospel ring loud through our evangelism and discipleship in our churches, and the lost in our communities will hear, see, and experience the gospel through a soul-winning church.

Praying, Posture, Preparing, Personal Evangelism, Preaching, and a Process for New Converts—these are the building blocks of a genuinely gospel-sharing culture. We sincerely hope that these biblical principles of a soul-winning church yield a harvest of gospel fruit in *your* church. We are praying for it—praying for you—as we finish up this conclusion. "Salvation belongs to the LORD."

PUTTING THE PRINCIPLES INTO PRACTICE

Some Case Studies

On the following pages you'll find the stories of churches who have thought through how to implement the six keys of this book in a way that has shaped their culture. You will find them all online too—simply head to the link below. And you can contribute the stories of your own church's life, in order to share ideas and inspiration with others, by emailing evangelisticculture@thegoodbook.com.

1. WHERE THE HARVEST BEGINS:
Pray for Conversions

Students in Prayer | Storyline Church in Arvada, Colorado, USA

When you walk into the student's area of Storyline Church, a giant board with a map of Arvada greets you. And this board shows every school that is either (1) near Storyline or (2) attended by Storyline students. They currently have 20 schools on their map, and the number of students in these schools totals 14,000.

The Student Minister, Morgan Marshall, shared how they are building a culture of evangelism and prayer for conversion with their students.

> *"We have 14,000 students in the Arvada area that we know need to hear the good news of the gospel. We present this as the mission field for our students. Last year, when our students entered into 6th grade (which is the beginning of our student ministry), they received a shirt that said, 'Arvada 14,000' on it, as a way to encourage them to be part of reaching every teen in our city/area. We also have stickers that our students and parents put on water bottles and computers as reminders to pray for the 14,000 students in Arvada. 14,000 is a special number in Colorado since we have over 50 mountains that are called '14er,' meaning they are over 14,000 feet. And so when we pray for the 14,000 students in Arvada, we are metaphorically asking God to move mountains! This has been helpful*

for our students to see how big this number is and how possible it is with God!"

Storyline also has a specific "mission moment" in each of their student gatherings. They take five to ten minutes before the teaching time for "prayer, care, and share." (This is language from the Dare 2 Share evangelistic ministry.) Examples of how they use this time include:

- dividing up by schools and praying specifically for their school, teachers, friends, and one another

- partnering up and praying for one another

- each student praying specifically for one friend whom they will see the next day at school who doesn't know the gospel

- praying for opportunities to share the gospel and for courage to take them

- sharing stories about friends they have invited and then praying together

- sharing stories of opportunities they have had to care for a friend

- sharing stories about opportunities to share the gospel with a friend

- practicing sharing the gospel together (using a variety of methods/strategies)

- having a student demonstrate sharing the gospel with the group

Storyline's heart for conversions is evident. And their plan is encouraging. Marshall said, "We try to point them [our students] specifically to praying for a specific friend and to seeing the whole picture of the 14,000 students in our area who need to hear the gospel."

An Evangelistic Event | The Church of Eleven 22 in Jacksonville, Florida, USA

The Church of Eleven 22 in Jacksonville, Florida organized an event known as "Saturate," a four-day revival-type meeting aimed at seeing countless conversions.

For Saturate, the entire church committed to fervent prayer, seeking the salvation of hundreds of souls. The event was saturated in prayer. Prayer teams were assembled to intercede for speakers, sermon preparation, and those who needed to find their way to the church. Buses bearing the revival's name and date traversed the city, inviting people to attend. The church leveraged social media to spread the word and encourage attendance. Throughout the event, nightly prayers were offered for God to save many, resulting in an increasing number of conversions each year. In 2021, 225 people came to faith, and in 2023, over 300 individuals professed faith in Jesus during Saturate.

2. BEFORE YOU SAY, "GO AND SHARE YOUR FAITH": The Posture of an Evangelistic Church

A Creative Podcast | The Well Church of Americus in Americus, Georgia, USA

John Schroeder planted The Well in the rural town of Americus, Georgia. From the beginning, he entered Americus with the posture of a listener, learner, and connector—which led to starting a podcast on his town, for his town.

"The Americus Podcast serves as a means to explore the culture of a town about which I knew little," says John. He knew the importance of relationships being a two-way street. And a missiological question led to him starting the podcast: "Understanding people, no matter where you find yourself, requires active listening. I didn't just want to live and do ministry here. I wanted to be a part of the town's history. So, how can I grow in love for a town I have never lived in?" The podcast is part of the answer.

"The podcast is designed," says John, "to spotlight the history, values, needs, and future aspirations of the city from the perspective of each guest. Essentially, it serves as an oral history, focusing on our guest's personal experiences, impact, and values and tying them to the larger cultural landscape and history of Americus/Sumter County."

John asks guests, who range from public officials to business owners and citizens:

1. Who are you?

2. What do you do?

3. Where is Americus going?

4. How, as neighbors, can we get there together?

In a short time, John has seen the podcast make a significant relational impact. "I doubt I would have established connections to this extent without this platform. The podcast was something I felt the Lord wanted me to do." He has used the podcast to open doors on- and off-air to share the gospel. John has been able to connect with guests away from the microphones, care for them, tell them about Jesus, and invite people to church. And John does all of this with a patience that is needed in church-planters and pastors:

"The Lord may use you to call someone to repentance and faith in the first conversation. Praise the Lord! But is your heart postured for the long haul of evangelism? I will see my neighbors and podcast guests at the local grocery store, the park, restaurants, or city events throughout the year. I hope to have more than one opportunity to share the gospel while being their friend. I am praying and making use of the time I have with each person, hoping not only to call them neighbors but also brothers or sisters."

Hospitality | Metro Life Church in Philadelphia, Pennsylvania, USA

When Metro Church launched in 2012, its primary desire was to reach nonbelievers in Greater Philadelphia, a commuter city that looks weary from the number of old church buildings on its corners. Philadelphia ranks among the highest cities (#17) in the country in terms of percentage of residents who are religiously unaffiliated.

How does a church even begin to establish an ongoing relationship with those not currently in the church? The pastoral team at Metro knew that they had to break away from old patterns of ministerial behavior that were driven by cultural influence, upbringing, or mere complacency. In God's hand, this posture was critical to Metro's sustained growth. Pastor Donny Cho says that "80% of Metro's congregants identified themselves as either 'unchurched' or 'de-churched' prior to coming to Metro." Metro Church defined a roadmap for effectively engaging with unbelievers or new converts, believing that every interaction was a pivotal opportunity to shape someone towards "rethinking Jesus" and "rethinking church."

Metro Church thought about their hospitality as a key to demonstrating love and connection.

- Metro places a premium on invitation. Donny says, "Today, most people are 'belongers' before they become 'believers.' This means our behavior must counter the expectation that people need to become Christians before they are 'in.'" At Metro, this means anyone can walk through the doors.

- The hospitality team at Metro assumes that every visitor is unchurched. "Most of our greeters and ushers," according to Donny, "are recent converts themselves, who more easily relate to what a visitor desires, fears, and needs." Metro has tasked specific leaders to work with the hospitality team in each service to actively engage with visitors. They make it a point to introduce visitors to people who may be similar in age, profession, marital status, or residential location.

- Interest or inquiries are often met with invitations to coffee or a meal, with a genuine desire to organically introduce visitors into a community of believers in the church, while simultaneously addressing any questions or preconceived notions about being a Christian or life in the church.

- For Donny and the leaders at Metro, it is important to stress that Sunday worship must also be evangelistic in nature. Cho says, "We are always focused on preaching to the unbeliever, and preaching that way addresses the unbelief in everyone." In addition to preaching, Metro thinks hard about use of undefined Christian jargon or inside jokes, which can alienate those that are new to the church.

3. SALT AND LIGHT: Preparing for Conversions

Laundry Love | Epiphany Baltimore in Baltimore, Maryland, USA
Under the leadership of Charlie Mitchell, the church started on a simple and practical evangelistic endeavor known as "Laundry Love."

This outreach initiative aimed to open up opportunities to evangelize by first demonstrating grace to the community. Armed with bags full of quarters, laundry detergent, bleach, dryer sheets, toys for children, food, and grills, church members went to laundromats across the city. Their mission was simple: to share love and compassion with people doing laundry. They generously paid for their laundry, engaged in conversations about the gospel, and showered people with affection. With music in the background and hot dogs sizzling on the grill, Epiphany Baltimore created a warm and inviting atmosphere.

Over the course of a year, Laundry Love allowed members to share the gospel with hundreds of individuals. This initiative made a meaningful impact on a community through small, affordable, and heartwarming gestures of kindness.

Parking Help | Epiphany Church in Wilmington, Delaware, USA

Epiphany Wilmington, led by Pastor Derrick Parks, creatively addressed the parking challenges of their densely populated city. They found a simple yet powerful way to connect with their community by putting quarters in parking meters to save others from receiving tickets. Their acts of kindness allowed them to engage in conversations about the gospel, offer prayers, introduce themselves, and invite people to worship services. These small gestures not only provided relief but also opened the door for countless people to encounter the gospel for the first time.

Minding the Gap | Sunday@Seven at St. Andrew's Kirk Ella, in East Yorkshire, UK

Hull is statistically one of the cities in the UK with the lowest churchgoing population by proportion. Most of its inhabitants wouldn't consider just walking into a church, even if invited by a friend.

"So we realized that we needed both to equip our members—who were older teens, college students, and young professionals—to share the gospel with their friends, and also to give them different opportunities to bring a friend to something that brought them into contact with our church community," says Carl Laferton, who was part of the team who started the evening congregation.

The leadership came across a course called Mind the Gap, and from that they developed different levels of events:

- A Level One event was one which simply gathered some of the community in an informal setting, with no gospel content other than conversation—for instance, a curry night or girls' night in. Members could bring their friends to experience the warmth and kindness of Christians being together.

- Level Two was a gathering where the draw was relational or social but there was some gospel content—for instance, a quiz night with a brief evangelistic talk.

- Level Three was an event at which the gospel content was front and center—a dinner where a few members shared their testimonies, or a "Grill-a-Christian" event at which a couple of church members who were confident in apologetics would answer any question anyone asked, or an evangelistic curriculum such as Christianity Explored.

The church aimed to hold at least one event at each level every month—and it worked:

"They brought us into contact with people who'd never have gone from zero to walking into church, and we saw many of those people starting to consider for themselves the claims of Christ.

"At the same time, we sought to ensure that our church services themselves were easy to access—we had a coffee time beforehand with things like foosball tables, air-hockey tables, and so on set up. And then the service itself aimed to contain no barriers other than the gospel. We tried always to ask ourselves, 'How does this feel to someone who's never been to church?' Of course there are things we do because the Bible directs us to, for the good of the Lord's people, that are strange to a visitor. And we'll be unashamed about doing them. But those things—the Lord's Supper, singing, and so on—are also invitations to show visitors that the gospel really matters, really changes us, and really anchors and comforts us.

"We were a small church service, but we saw a real fostering of a culture of evangelism—people inviting friends, those friends coming to Christ, and then a renewed confidence in making Jesus known to others."

4. TELLING PEOPLE JESUS IS AWESOME: Personal Evangelism

Ready to Answer | Cornerstone Church Liverpool in Liverpool, UK

When it comes to personal evangelism, the apostle Peter's charge to "always be prepared to give an answer to everyone who asks you to give the reason for the hope that you have" (1 Peter 3:15, NIV) has been the most defining verse for Steve and Siân Robinson of Cornerstone Church Liverpool.

Peter wrote these words, Steve points out, to remind Christians to be prepared to talk about Christ as they live their Christianity in the ordinariness of life in the context of a hostile or indifferent culture. This intentionality isn't only about frequenting the places where nonbelievers do life, like the gym or the local pub. This gospel intentionality means living the reality of their own lives as Christians in front of unbelievers.

The Robinsons have walked many years of suffering with their eldest daughter, Ella, who has had numerous health problems. Living through suffering in front of their nonbelieving friends has invited questions and conversations. People ask, "How do you cope? Where do you get your strength?" The Robinsons give their answer: Jesus.

Steve and Siân are convinced that it is only as they live with a gospel honesty in front of nonbelieving friends and family that those around them will see the hope they have in Jesus. The Robinsons have seen several friends, family, neighbors, and coworkers of Siân come to know Jesus. The suffering that they have walked through has led to conversations about their Savior—and to conversions to their Savior.

Commissioned to Cast | New Heights Church in Milton, West Virginia, USA

Jesus told his disciples that he would turn them into fishers of men (Matthew 4:19, ESV). That's the end result of evangelism. The first step is casting the net. As Will Basham, pastor of New Heights Church, thought about how their church approaches evangelism, he realized that you can't become an effective fisherman without first learning how to cast. "Unfortunately, much of our evangelism training focuses on later parts of evangelism, when in reality, most people get stuck on casting—the very first step!" While most of the church's members could articulate and share the gospel, they had no clue about how to get gospel conversations started. "Our church members couldn't cast!"

New Heights Church decided to teach members how to get from everyday conversations to gospel conversations. "Good questions," says Will, "are like the 'casting' of evangelism." Most Christians find it easier ask good questions than make bold statements. And it's also true that when those questions are asked rightly, space for bold gospel presentations opens up. Because New Heights Church is in a context where many consider themselves Christian or religious, one easy question has generated many gospel conversations: "Is there anything I can help you pray about today?" From this one question, Will says, "I've heard so many stories of people coming to Christ and plugging into our church simply because one of our members began praying for a need in their life. That question leads to prayer, which leads to follow-up, which leads to gospel opportunities."

New Heights Church has discipled their people into using the simple questions below as ways to cast a line and hopefully move conversations toward talking about Jesus:

- How have you and your family been doing?

- What are you getting into this weekend?

- Do you have a church that you're a part of?

- Do you have any spiritual beliefs?

- Do you pray? Would you mind praying for me?

The question-casting has become a regular part of the church's culture. At the end of every Sunday service, a pastor commissions the Christians to go and cast. New Heights believes that every week, all of their members should be sent out as missionaries. And this commissioning has its own section in the liturgy. Will explains how this works:

"*Each Sunday, one of our pastors will remind us that we're not 'dismissed from service,' but rather we are 'commissioned to service.' He calls us to spend our entire week looking for opportunities to ask questions like these that lead to gospel conversations, and we always end our service with three powerful words: 'You are sent.'*"

Making and Taking Opportunities | Living Hope Church, Inverness, Scotland

According to Pete Rennie, pastor of Living Hope Church, "Evangelism in the Scottish Highlands is easy because around 98% of people don't know Jesus." When believers join Living Hope Church, they are brought up to speed on the plan to reach their community. "Our evangelistic strategy is you!" Pete tells them. But while Living Hope Church wants their members to see themselves as missionaries in the places where they live, work, and play, Pete is honest with himself too. "As the pastor of our church, I see myself as the lead-evangelist in our church. If I'm not living evangelistically, why should I expect any of our members to be?" Personal evangelism—making and taking opportunities—is modeled by the Rennie family.

This conviction led Pete and his wife to purchase a house right in the middle of a brand new suburb in the west of Inverness, the area their church is seeking to reach with the good news of Jesus Christ. Pete decided to make opportunities for evangelism: "We decided that we'd be the 'weirdos' who would cross the road to introduce ourselves. I soon found out that I'd become known as the guy who waves at everyone!" The Rennies wanted to be hospitable and friendly neighbors, so they began hosting street barbecues, lighting a fire pit on their drive for toasting marshmallows at Halloween, dropping goody bags at their neighbors' doors, hiding Easter eggs in the garden on Easter Sunday, and inviting neighbors over for food each Christmas. Pete adds, "My wife deserves all the credit for this. We also bought a dog as soon as we moved into our house so that we're regularly seen walking in the neighborhood. I am even a part of the community council."

In addition to following their own evangelistic routines, the Rennies also take opportunities for gospel conversations. Pete and his wife try to support community initiatives like the annual street Christmas-light switch-on. Living Hope's band has been invited to play at the event. "All of these things," says Pete, "provide avenues for us to meet people who don't know Jesus yet."

While some aspects of evangelism in the Scottish Highlands are easy, it is also difficult because in this post-Christian context most of the people the Rennies encounter are at best indifferent to Jesus and at worst hostile to him: "I've found that, while initially we had lots of conversations about Jesus, particularly as people asked about my job, over time those conversations dried up as people learnt to avoid this topic by avoiding asking me questions." This means that the long work of personal evangelism for the Rennies has involved a lot of prayer, introducing neighbors to other Christians, inviting people to evangelistic events at their church, and a big dose of patience. "After eight years of this long work, we are encouraged to see God using our efforts with a number of our neighbors accepting invitations to church events and asking really good questions about Jesus." The Rennies are also seeing others in their church follow their patient example of taking and making opportunities for gospel conversations.

5. SIX QUESTIONS: Preaching and Teaching for Conversion

Preaching with Unbelievers in Mind | Living Stones Church in Sparks, Nevada, USA

Living Stones Church has grown to a family of nine churches throughout northern Nevada—a context that continually tops the list as the least churched state in the USA. 2020 census data shows Nevada has the least number of churches per person compared to the rest of the 50 states. And for the leaders of Living Stones, this presents a ripe opportunity for reaching and preaching to unbelievers and new Christians. "At one point, not too long ago," says pastor Mark South, "50% of Living Stones attendees had no previous church background and had become Christians at a Living Stones church." These stats in and outside the church have encouraged Mark to think about how he preaches to unbelievers in the room. "In our context, our church is always mindful of the unbelievers sitting in the seats on any Sunday morning." Mark South shared six things he intentionally thinks through when preaching at Living Stones:

1. Define and defend language and concepts with simplicity and clarity. South recognizes that much of our Christian vocabulary is not understood by those outside the church. And while there was never a time when society was genuinely Christian, there were contexts where words like "theology" needed no explanation.

"A preacher must go above and beyond to avoid making assumptions about agreed-upon concepts." He takes time to explain essential words and considers how an unbeliever may hear certain words.

2. The sermon must be human. Preachers must work hard to discover the shared experiences of being human, whether the listener is a Christian or not. How does this passage connect to the unbeliever's real-life experience? Mark thinks as he prepares, "What are the effects of the world's fallenness on those listening to this sermon, and how does this sermon address them?"

3. The preacher must be human. "Authenticity," says Mark, "is the currency of influence." Mark considers how the text is personally changing and challenging him. Christians and non-Christians can tell whether someone's preaching portrays that he lives in the real world or in a fantasy land detached from reality. Mark wants his sermons to demonstrate that he is "experiencing the same frustrations and disappointments as everyone else."

4. Applications determine the extent of actual understanding. Preachers shouldn't spend 99% of the sermon on exegesis and 1% on application. Every part of the sermon matters. Mark wants to think through all of his applications. "Most

preachers apply a text by making general theoretical or theological applications that sound good—but are they helpful to a single mom surviving on Monday morning?" Mark challenges himself to be preaching in the real world, not the library.

5. Deal with opposition in the sermon. Biblically sound sermons ought to present some form of opposition in the listeners' minds. The gospel is a rock of offense. God's truth goes against the grain of sinful flesh. Mark considers and answers opposition in the mind and the heart to what is being said. "Of course, I cannot handle every sort of opposition, but for every point I preach, I will think of a specific way an outsider might struggle with what I am saying."

6. Set out a specific pathway of response to every sermon. The weekly liturgy at Living Stones includes communion after the sermon. This creates a moment for believers and unbelievers. "At the end of every sermon, the clear response pathway for the Christian is communion." And for the unbeliever in the room, this means an invitation to pray or meet with the response team. The response team is there "for the unbeliever who has questions or is experiencing a desire to trust in Jesus." Then, before sharing the bread and wine, Living Stones will take a

moment to celebrate any new convert who is about to participate in their first communion. It is a moment that can be used by God to highlight his grace and draw others to himself. These moments create opportunities for reflection for everyone in the room: "What do I believe?"

Three Areas to Think Through | Redemption City Church in Baltimore, Maryland, USA

Baltimore is not the Bible Belt. The city's crime rate and the percentage of people who have never heard of Jesus are both higher than in many cities in North America. Old church buildings in Baltimore are now coffee shops and yoga studios. Baltimore is a post-Christian context. Pastor Adam Muhtaseb says he thinks about three simple focus areas for himself as he aims to preach for conversions: relevance, relatability, and radiance.

1. Thinking through Relevance

Biblical preaching is always rooted in the text of Scripture. The Bible is the source material for sermons that pack genuine power. Adam thinks about preaching in a way that shows the relevance of the text and of Christ to the lives of his hearers. This doesn't mean ignoring the realities of unbelievers in the room. He thinks about finding their values, heroes, desires, and hurts, and connecting them to the gospel. He seeks to leave "breadcrumbs" for the unbelievers in the room:

*"I often analyze the popular elements of culture
and show that the reason why these creations have
universal appeal is because they universally point us
to a truth endowed in us by our Creator. For example,
I might say something like 'J Cole, the famous rapper,
has a famous song called "Pride Is the Devil" and that's
actually the main point of our text in Proverbs 8.' It's
short. It's simple. But it gives unbelievers handles to
grab onto God's word. How can you meet people where
they are, grab them by the hand, and lead them across
the bridge to Christ?"*

2. Thinking through Relatability

Adam knows that unbelievers may feel a giant disconnect between the preacher and themselves. In some ways, this is unavoidable and warranted. Unbelievers are, after all, still dead in their sins. But we are all still humans in need of God's grace. Preachers can declare and demonstrate the power of the gospel from the story of Scripture and the story of their lives:

*"The gospel is powerful not just coming from a
preacher but through a preacher. I try to say things
like 'Here's what God's word says... Here's where
we fail. In fact here's where I've failed... But here's
the good news of what Jesus has done...' That's
the beginnings of a great sermon. When I bring my
real pain, my real doubts, my real struggles to the
forefront for people to see, and present them with
the real hope that Jesus is sufficient in all that*

mess, that's guaranteed to stick with an unbeliever.
Actually sharing your life and the gospel's real impact
has always been my bread-and-butter in leading
unbelievers to Jesus Christ."

3. Thinking through Radiance

There is a kind of preaching that captures people's attention not because of rhetorical skill or flourish, nor appearance or personality, but because of what Adam calls "radiance"—what preachers of the past called unction: a kind of power in preaching that only comes by prayer and the power of the Spirit. "You can't manufacture radiance," says Adam. "You can't practice in the mirror and create it. It comes not from gritting your teeth but falling on your knees. It comes when the text is speaking to you as much as it's speaking to others. It's the natural overflow of a real intimacy with Jesus Christ."

Adam thinks about preaching as proclamation and participation. It is the preacher proclaiming and sitting under the proclamation. The preacher needs to be set on fire first by the truths he's preaching. "If unbelievers can sense that you've been with God, they just may want to meet the God they sense you know," as he puts it.

6. THE BEGINNING, NOT THE END: A Process for New Converts

An Organic Plan | Metro Life Church in Philadelphia, Pennsylvania, USA

As Metro Life Church thought about their process for new converts, they realized that the key there, as for all churches, is discipleship. And Metro tries to balance the structured and the organic aspects of discipleship. "Rather than relying on a program that involves a few leaders," says Pastor Donny Cho, "we foster a culture of organic relationships that are focused on spiritual renewal and maturity." This includes the following examples from Metro Life Church, which may be helpful for your church:

A Visitors' Luncheon on a Regular Basis
- Someone coming to faith in Jesus or new to the church can intentionally connect over this lunch with a pastor, small-group facilitator, and other leaders.

- Invitations and recommendations are subsequently made for small groups (geographical), fellowships (life-stage based), or additional church gatherings.

- In most cases, new friends or leaders accompany visitors to this meal as a part of growing together.

Small Groups, Fellowship Groups, and Even Outreach Opportunities

- The content, training, or dialogue in each group is always intended to move people towards gospel-centered application.

- Every ministry in the church, in essence, is viewed with the outcome of nurturing real discipleship relationships—ultimately, providing multiple ways of bringing the gospel to people in the church.

Worship and Service in the Church

- As a new Christian participates in Sunday worship, connects with a small group, and serves the local community, they are able to talk about what they're learning, thinking about, and struggling with with new friends and leaders in the church at a regular pace.

- Additional opportunities in the church become available to shape the person in the foundational truths of the gospel, enable the congregant to plug into the life of the community, and teach the individual the core values of the local body. New members participate in adult Christian education classes, membership and baptism classes, and further opportunities to serve in the church.

As a church, Metro regularly encourages its congregation at large through testimonies, prayer, invitations, and stories of renewal that shape the life of the congregation. Today, over 50% of its current lay leadership consists of people who were not even in any church prior to attending Metro. The missional focus of its people and a culture of discipleship continue to lead to authentic relationships that nurture spiritual maturity, particularly among new converts.

New and Misled Believers | Igreja do Redentor in Rio De Janeiro, Brazil

Igreja do Redentor (Church of the Redeemer) exists in a city where broadly "evangelical" churches have seen significant growth, yet the vast majority are not gospel-centered. Pastor Cristiano Gaspar says, "Many are extremely legalistic, preaching salvation through good deeds"—and one of the fastest-growing groups in Brazil is the one promoting prosperity theology. Cristiano divides these into two streams: "First are those promising material wealth. And they are growing mainly among the lower-middle and lower classes. Second are the churches promising personal success, portraying Jesus as a consultant for personal achievement and emotional issue resolution."

It's in this challenging context that Church of the Redeemer is thinking through discipleship. In addition to expository preaching, ongoing theology classes, and small groups, Church of the Redeemer has a specific discipleship process for new converts and believers from these kinds of non-gospel-based church backgrounds:

"Initially, we put new believers and those from legalistic churches or prosperity backgrounds through two discipleship classes. The first is the 'Fundamentals' class, lasting two months. Here, we discuss the doctrinal foundations of the Christian faith, explaining who God is, the person of Jesus, and the person of the Holy Spirit. We talk about how the Bible is the word of God. And we explain the role of the church in a Christian's life. We also cover creation, fall, redemption, and consummation."

After this survey of foundational theology, their next class takes people through the book *The Gospel-Centered Life* by Robert H. Thune and Will Walker: "We believe this book greatly aids in understanding how the gospel shapes a believer's life. The gospel is essential not only at the start but throughout the Christian journey."

After these two classes, people take a shorter class called "Chapter 1." This class focuses on Church of the Redeemer's ecclesiology and history as a local church: "Here, those who have moved through the previous classes and those believers who have moved from healthy churches meet one another." And it's in this class that the church's membership covenant is signed, with unbaptized believers being led toward baptism before signing.

APPENDIX ONE:

A Liturgy for the Lost

Father, Son, and Spirit, We confess today as your redeemed ones:
[All] **Salvation belongs to the Lord.**

We have many around us who don't know you and your saving power. For them, we ask: **Save them, Lord.**

We have neighbors, coworkers, family, and friends who do not know you and your heart, which is ready to forgive. For them, we ask: **Forgive them, Lord.**

We know people who have yet to find the joy of knowing you, Jesus. They need your death and resurrection. For them we ask: **Convert them, Lord.**

We have tasted and seen that you are good: a God mighty to save. We want to tell of all your gracious works and words. We ask: **Use us, Lord!**

May the songs we sing, the words we offer in prayer, and

the sermon we hear from your divine word be used to exalt the Savior as he draws sinners to himself. We say as your people: **Salvation belongs to the Lord.**

APPENDIX TWO:

Areas to Cover with New Believers

Here's a starter list of topics to cover with a new convert. Be sure to look at what the Bible says on each topic. This could be done in regular meetings over coffee, or through a class or small group. This list is by no means exhaustive or in a concrete order. We hope this will stir up ideas for training new converts.

- *The Bible:* God's word and its truth and trustworthiness; its nature in illuminating and providing spiritual food; the story of Scripture and how it all points to Jesus.

- *Spiritual Disciplines:* How to read the Bible; how to pray; fasting; pursuing Christ-likeness. Model this area by reading, meditating, and praying through a book of the Bible together.

- *Doctrines of God:* The Trinity; the attributes of God.

- *Christ:* The deity and humanity of Jesus; the titles of Jesus; the love of Jesus; the work of Jesus in his incarnation, death, resurrection, ascension, and present reign and intercession.

- *The Holy Spirit:* The gifts and fruit of the Spirit; the power of the Spirit in the Christian life.

- *Humanity:* Creator and creature distinction; what it means to be made in the image of God, with dignity; what it means to be male and female, and live in community.

- *Sin:* The fall; temptation; indwelling sin; Satan; how to put sin to death by the Spirit.

- *Gospel Fruits:* Faith; the golden chain (justification, sanctification, glorification); good works.

- *Church:* The nature of the church; the leadership of the church (elders and deacons, etc.); membership of the church; the ordinances of the church (baptism and Lord's Supper); church as a "one-anothering" community; the gathering of the church (sermons, singing, giving, and so on).

- *Identity in Christ:* Gospel centrality; union with Christ; new creation; our status as forgiven, holy, loved children of God.

- *Last Things:* Heaven and hell; the return of Christ; the new Jerusalem.

- *Cultural flashpoints:* Gender; marriage; expressive individualism; greed; sexuality; and so on.

- *Evangelism:* How to share a personal testimony; how to share the gospel.

ACKNOWLEDGMENTS

From Jeff:

To the unknown preacher—the man who faithfully proclaimed the reality of sin, hell, and the gospel at a children's camp in the early 1990s—thank you. I'm so thankful you invited us little sinners to trust Jesus. To the counselor at the camp, probably a parent volunteering, who told me what it means to be a Christian—thank you.

I must thank my coauthor, Uncle Doug. Your friendship in and outside of writing is one of the great blessings in my life. It was an honor to work on this book with you. There is no way either of us could have imagined that a phone call about training pastors and planters would grow into a book. Your wisdom and insight made it exponentially better. You will forever be the master of illustrations—no one has stories and a gospel spidey sense like Doug Logan.

To Paul Tripp, thank you for graciously writing the foreword and giving your encouragement and support to our writing. I don't have enough room to share how your ministry has refreshed me over and over in the ocean of grace. I thank God for you.

Thanks to Carl Laferton and The Good Book Company. Your edits and excitement over our book helped keep the writing engine running. Your overhauls and fine-tuning made our writing stronger. I'm grateful.

Thanks to all the churches and pastors who allowed us to share how they are laboring to be soul-winning churches. I was inspired and encouraged by your contributions to the book. May your tribe—and converts—increase!

Thanks to Oliver, Ivy, and Natalie for encouraging me to just keep writing whenever and wherever. Many soccer and basketball practices provided many words. And thanks for cheering Doug and me on as we talked on the phone... a lot.

And unending thanks to our soul-winning Savior. This book is an extended prayer to the one who delights in saving sinners. Do your thing, Jesus.

From Doug:

In crafting this book, I find myself profoundly indebted to my esteemed cowriter, Jeff Medders (Neffew). I am truly honored to have embarked on this journey with such a talented cowriter. I extend my deepest gratitude for the countless hours of shared passion, dedication, and intellectual exchange that have shaped the very essence of every page of this book. The collaborative synergy we've cultivated has not only enriched the content but also enhanced the overall experience of bringing this project to fruition. I want to express my appreciation for your patience during the writing process and your enthusiasm, which fueled our shared inspiration, and your unwavering belief in the vision we set out to create. I'm honored that you would ever consider me a spiritual uncle.

A heartfelt thank-you to Olivia Meade (Big Country), my creative editor, whose discerning eye and insightful suggestions breathed life into my writing. Your dedication to refining the narrative and enhancing its gospel clarity has been invaluable. This book bears the imprint of your editorial craftsmanship, and I am sincerely thankful for the expertise and passion you brought to every edit.

To the amazing members of the Remnant Church RVA, thank you for entrusting me with the great responsibility of shepherding your souls. Thank you for your unwavering support and warm embrace of Angel, myself, and our entire family as I took on the role of

Pastor for Church Planting in 2018. Your beautiful faith and commitment to the gospel have been tremendous inspiration and encouragement. I am also indebted to the elders, deacons, and ministry leaders of Remnant Church RVA for your commitment to the mission of the church—your passion for reaching out to the lost has genuinely made this community a soul-winning church.

Thanks to Tye Tribbett and Thaddeus Tribbett, who were instrumental in leading me to Christ at my barber shop in South Jersey. I am ever grateful for your obedience to Christ and your passion to see this filthy unbeliever come to know Jesus.

I give all praise, honor, and glory to the eternal and ultimate soul-winner, Jesus the Christ. His guidance and beautiful presence fueled every chapter. By the sovereignty of my great God and King, we took on this endeavor, knowing it's ultimately all about advancing his kingdom. May this book be a vessel for Christ's truth to reach and transform lives. Thank you, Jesus, for being the true author of soul-winning and the founder of your soul-winning church, against which the gates of Hades will never prevail.

I dedicate this book to three young family members whom I pray God will raise up to be soul-winners at a soul-winning church: my grandson, London Reign Logan; my great-grandson, Jovanni Adi'yan Mendez-Rivera; and my nephew, David Logan Cho.

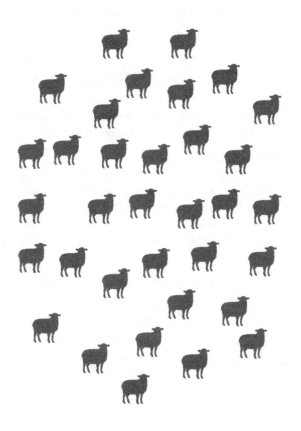

BIBLICAL | RELEVANT | ACCESSIBLE

At The Good Book Company, we are dedicated to helping Christians and local churches grow. We believe that God's growth process always starts with hearing clearly what he has said to us through his timeless word—the Bible.

Ever since we opened our doors in 1991, we have been striving to produce Bible-based resources that bring glory to God. We have grown to become an international provider of user-friendly resources to the Christian community, with believers of all backgrounds and denominations using our books, Bible studies, devotionals, evangelistic resources, and DVD-based courses.

We want to equip ordinary Christians to live for Christ day by day, and churches to grow in their knowledge of God, their love for one another, and the effectiveness of their outreach.

Call us for a discussion of your needs or visit one of our local websites for more information on the resources and services we provide.

Your friends at The Good Book Company

thegoodbook.com | thegoodbook.co.uk
thegoodbook.com.au | thegoodbook.co.nz
thegoodbook.co.in